D1554698

With his powerful memoir, *Transforming Manhood*, Ryan Sallans has provided the world with a true gift. With each chapter, Sallans bares his soul with intention, vulnerability, and power. In doing so, he invites the reader in to not only his gender journey, but also to delve into our assumptions about our own gender assumptions. This memoir stands along with the great ones — Leslie Feinberg's *Stone Butch Blues* and Michelle Obama's *Becoming*. With each page, there is tenderness, respect, and love even beyond our gender journeys that readers will feel for this thing we call "life." Sallans has issued a call for us to truly *live* our lives while we can. I didn't want the book to end, and that alone is one of the messages Sallans leaves the reader with about our own lives. A true gem!

> —Anneliese Singh, PhD, LPC
> Professor and Associate Dean of Diversity, Equity, and Inclusion, University of Georgia, and author of *The Racial Healing Handbook* and *The Queer and Transgender Resilience Workbook*

Ryan Sallans' *Transforming Manhood* is not just about contemporary trans issues, but about the human issues associated with human transformation such as mortality, finding peace and love within oneself, facing and accepting fear, and the complexity of family as a work in progress. Sallans is at his most vulnerable. While his "scars from the gender-affirming surgeries have faded, some now unseen," his story is his body, a beautiful "trail map of life's journey."

> —Loren Kleinman, *If I Don't Make It, I Love You*

We learn in *Transforming Manhood* that Ryan K. Sallans comes to us not as a *trail-blazer* but a trail *maintainer*. And that he does—honoring the generations of transgender people that came before him, inviting us to carry on the legacy of fighting for the rights of every person to live with pride and confidence in their true gender, with full support from those around them and compassion for those not yet there. With openness, empathy, brilliant insight, and a wide-angle lens, Sallans shares his personal journey from little girl to lesbian to trans man to human being. No other writer has come close to giving us a window into that evolutionary process, including the beginning of ageing—never a walk in the park but always bursting with new discoveries. A must read for anyone who wants to know, both inside and outside, what transgender looks like from transition to transformation to integration of all that we are that makes us mindful human beings.

> —Diane Ehrensaft, Ph.D.
> Author of *The Gender Creative Child* and *Gender Born, Gender Made* Director of Mental Health, Child and Adolescent Gender Center, University of California San Francisco

To read Ryan Sallans' new memoir, *Transforming Manhood: A Trans Man's Quest to Build Bridges and Knock Down Walls*, is to understand what it is to be a transgender man of Generation X, an activist sandwiched between the legendary (and, more often now, deceased) pioneers of the Baby Boomer generation and the Millennials. Does it matter? Most certainly.

> —Diane Anderson-Minshall
> Editorial Director of *The Advocate*
> Author of *Queerly Beloved: A Love Story Across Genders* and four novels

TRANSFORMING
MANHOOD

A TRANS MAN'S QUEST TO BUILD
BRIDGES AND KNOCK DOWN WALLS

RYAN K. SALLANS

TRANSFORMING
MANHOOD

Scout Publishing, LLC
P.O. Box 31214
Omaha, NE 68131
scoutpublishingllc.com

Edited by Stephanie Finnegan
Designed by Erika L. Block
Front Cover Photo by Aidan Faiella / Faiella Studios
Interior Photos by Fred Schneider, Melanie Rose-Smith and Hunter Lea

PUBLISHER'S CATALOGING-IN-PUBLICATION DATA:

Name: Sallans, Ryan K., author.

Title: Transforming manhood : a trans man's quest to build bridges
               and knock down walls / Ryan K. Sallans.

Description: Omaha, NE : Scout Publishing, LLC, [2019]

Identifiers: ISBN: 978-0-9895868-7-0 | 978-0-9895868-6-3 (ebook)

Subjects:

LCSH: Sallans, Ryan K. | Transgender men--Biography. | Transgender people--Biography. | Gender identity. | Transgender people--Violence against. | Eating disorders. | Men-- Psychology. | Masculinity--Psychological aspects. | Husbands--Psychological aspects. | Sons--Psychological aspects. | Self-esteem in men. | Self-confidence. | Middle age-- Psychological aspects. | Gay and lesbian studies. | LCGFT: Autobiographies. | BISAC: BIOGRAPHY & AUTOBIOGRAPHY / LGBT. | PSYCHOLOGY / Psychopathology / Eating Disorders. | SELF-HELP / Gender & Sexuality.

Classification: LCC: HQ77.8.S25 S252 2019 | DDC: 306.76--dc23

This memoir is based on my experiences over a fifteen-year period. In some instances, a name has been changed, characters have been combined, and events compressed. For the sake of the story and expediency, some dialogue and conversations have been imaginatively re-created, but are intended to portray events and experiences in my life.

TRANSFORMATION

In typography, a glyph is an elemental symbol within an agreed set of symbols, intended to represent a readable character for the purposes of writing. Throughout history, science, and spirituality, the symbol above has represented transformation.

TABLE OF CONTENTS

IN MEMORY OF KAREN MILLER AND GRANDMA TRIPLETT:

No matter my physicality, from anorexic to "healthy," from female to male, you were always there to support me. I miss you every day that passes.

The numbers you see above are chronological steps, representing months in my transitional journey.

PROLOGUE

SELFIES-SHAPING MAN

The past fifteen years of my life have been centered on my identity as a trans man, a person who was born assigned female, but transitioned to male. My survival has been propelled by a whirlwind of emotions and endless selfies documenting the changes that took place when my estrogen-based body was introduced to testosterone. Headshots, lined up side by side, numbering 1 to 168, show the monthly process of both aging and the dramatic effects of testosterone over the years. With each photo, there is an underlying story influenced by a string of events to get my life and body to that point. In some pictures, my skin has a glow that radiates a story of receiving good news, falling in love, or hearing words of validation from my family. In other photos, my face looks gaunt, due to loss, feelings of failure, questioning relevancy, or other hardships that happen because of life—or because my life includes being transgender.

Along with these selfies, my nude body has become a trail map of my life's journey and what I have created. My scars from the gender-affirming surgeries have faded, some now unseen. On my chest, where they removed the breasts (I don't like to refer to them as "my breasts"), the scars are a light pink and covered with a growing number of chest hairs. On my abdomen—on either side of my belly button—the two tiny slits used by the scopes to snip and clip the ovaries, fallopian tubes, and uterus are invisible. Several inches below my belly button, the circular scar, where a catheter tube exited my body after lower surgery, now looks like a scar formed by a child's scratched chicken pox.

△

In the past, I would scrutinize the parts of my body that were still viewed as female, from breasts, to hips, to the lack of having a penis. I couldn't get past those features and felt constant screaming in my head, begging to be freed from the pieces that did not belong. After going through surgery after surgery, and having my body absorb testosterone week after week, I have freed myself from that female shell that was not mine. When my body morphed from female to male, what began as a young baby-cheeked face turned into a hard, hairy, maturing . . . man's. As my body shifts, so does my knowledge on what it means to be transgender. This knowledge is highly sought after, but with maturation you begin to grapple with a new transition in life, navigating generational differences and the values placed on the young over the old.

My midlife crisis has officially begun. As I blow out the candles in the shape of a 4 and 0 on my birthday cake, I am far too aware of Father Time standing behind me. Instead of counting new chin hairs forming on my face, I am counting the number of gray hairs that have replaced my brown strands on the top of my head, and the number of hairs that I've lost on my crown and temples. Instead of being excited by my face changing with each injection of testosterone (so that I didn't look like I was twelve), I am now assessing the depth of my crow's feet and the wrinkles on my forehead. More and more frequently, I am coming to terms with assorted youth telling me, "You're the same age as my parents." Or, ignoring me altogether because they see me as just "some white dude."

The passage of time has taught me that how people see and interact with me changes with each decade, making it hard to find a place of stability. When I was a kid in the small farming town of Aurora, Nebraska, I was Dr. Sallans's daughter. After leaving my small town for college, I became the patient with an eating disorder. In graduate school, I was the newly out lesbian. Then came postcollege, where I became "trans man Ryan." Now, my transition and the years that have followed have pushed me up against the word "man." With this change, I am trying to figure out how I fit within those three little letters, while navigating the world and assumptions that surround me.

PART ONE

INVISIBILITY: DOES SOCIETY EVER WANT TO SEE, HEAR, AND SPEAK WITH TRANS MEN?

Being transgender, you quickly see how messaging around gender deeply impacts our understanding of self and expression, and also how quickly society can push you into the box it feels most comfortable with constructing. What we need to understand is that a given label and the associated box do not define a person, but rather confine them.

—Ryan K. Sallans

CHAPTER 1

GENDER IS FAKE!

Selfie 131 – March 2016

The room was large for such a small group. If I was the organizer, I would have wanted a different space, a place where you could feel concealed, but also free enough to crawl around in your own skin when you felt uncomfortable. Plastic chairs were mixed in with chairs on wheels, haphazardly forming a lazy circle; some held bodies, others were left unoccupied, representing those who couldn't come or who were afraid to face what they wanted to escape. I was invited to join the support group that night, a group for college students from first year to graduate school to come together and talk about their gender identities and forms of expression.

Ten years ago, if I had been invited to this type of group, it most likely would have been held for folks who identified as either trans men or trans women. Now I sat in a room of fourteen people, and ten out of the fourteen students identified as nonbinary, meaning they weren't aligning with being a man or a woman. Rather, they presented as either something outside of these identities, in between, or a combination of both. I was invited to join them before giving a talk on their campus that evening. It is an invitation I take seriously, since I am the outlier joining a private space where students share some of their most vulnerable feelings.

Like with many groups I have been invited to, the beginning was awkward. I felt a little bit ignored as the students began conducting check-ins by talking about their week. They avoided looking at me as they talked. I continued sitting there, listening, and wondering if maybe they didn't want this stranger in their safe space. The students finished going around the circle, and then all eyes in the room turned toward me. Everyone sat silently. The energy in the room paused.

Oh, I thought, *I am supposed to share, too.* "My name is Ryan, I am thirty-six years old . . ."

". . . You could be one of my parents!" My share was interrupted by one of the students.

I looked over at the student who was smiling and scanning my whole body. It is interesting working with college students—each year, they stay the same age, but you continue to get older. When I hear that I'm the same age as their parents, or that students were born the same year I graduated from college, I am reminded how fast this life goes. I am also reminded that being someone who transitioned in 2005, I now have an invisible badge of honor that has pushed me into the position of being a statesman to any person who is exploring gender or starting a transition.

"Wow . . . cool," I replied before clearing my throat and continuing, "My week has been fine . . . I'm just tired of winter." *That was a terrible share, Ryan,* I thought as everyone sat in silence. It was one of those pauses in conversation where no one really knew what to say next; as the length of time spent in silence grew, so did everyone's discomfort. Fortunately, the lull was broken by the door to the classroom swinging open. Swooping in with the gust of wind from the entryway, and leaving a trailing smell of perfume, was a young trans woman with fresh makeup on her face.

"Sorry, sorry . . . I know I am late," she said. As she sat down, I could feel the shyness in the room melt. Her energy calmed the other students; I could tell they all looked up to her.

"It's okay," a trans man, sitting to my right, responded. "We were just finishing up our check-ins for the week. How has your week been?"

"My week was fine . . . except . . . someone in my class today used the word 'transsexual.'" Her arms wrapped around her torso, and her right leg flung up over her left before slowly beginning to bounce up and down.

"Ugh," another student sighed as they began to squirm on the hard-plastic seat.

"Yuck, that word isn't even used here in the United States," another student said to help the others who felt uncomfortable. "I think it is only used in France . . . or something."

A small chuckle leaked out of me at that moment; I couldn't help myself, or hold it in. All of the students looked at me, curious to know what was so funny. Hearing them, I realized how quickly generations can change, and how their understandings of life, identity, and language can be very different. For me, "transsexual" was a word that contained everything that created my identity prior to my transition. It began when I touched the pages of Loren Cameron's book *Body Alchemy: Transsexual Portraits*, and continued when the publishers that created *Original Plumbing Magazine* had T-shirts with *Nobody Knows I Am a Transsexual* printed across the front. The word "transsexual" was a part of us, but with younger generations it had been pushed to the sideline as something that was not appropriate. While I am fully aware and supportive of expanding language, I am also very aware of how we can marginalize one another when we tell others what words they can or cannot use in regard to their own identities.

"Okay, everyone, it's time for a history lesson," I said. All the students sat quiet, open to listening to the guy who was as old as their parents. "While there is a debate about who coined it, the word 'transsexual' was first used by Magnus Hirschfeld, a German doctor who was one of the pioneers of trans medicine, in 1923. Its origin came from the root word 'trans,' which in Latin means 'across'—so to be transsexual means 'across sexes.'" I paused to see if they were still following me. All eyes seemed locked onto my face, and their ears on my words. "When I first came out in 2005, 'transsexual' was the word many of us used who were seeking or had begun a physical transition." Some students began to shake their heads, and from their expressions, I could tell they didn't understand why someone would want to use *that* word. I quickly likened it to the word "queer," one that some people find empowering and all-encompassing, and others find to be a harmful reminder of them being hurt by those who could not, or would not, accept their identity. I felt the air lift a little in the room as the students processed the differences in language and how it is used.

"But what is the difference between gender identity and gender expression?" asked a student, born assigned male, who was wearing red lipstick and had nail polish on their fingernails.

"A person's gender identity is related to our psychological identification with a gender. For example, I was born assigned female, but my gender identity is male, so I was able to use hormones and surgery to align my body with my brain. Gender expression is how we feel comfortable expressing forms of gender, from clothing to makeup, to even how we talk."

"I get so upset with my mom when she says, 'You're such a boy,'" the same student said, sounding exasperated. "I guess I just get confused because I don't feel like a boy, but then she says things like that."

"Ugh. . . ," another student, born assigned female, responded before letting out a huge exhale of frustrated air. "Ryan . . . when will *I know* if I am a boy?"

This student's question will forever be bookmarked in my brain. When I feel frustrated with youth who are angry, or youth who attack people who have a different way of describing their identity, I'll let this student's voice enter into my memory. The energy behind the question showed the fear and frustration that youth have with gender identity development. It showed that youth today are in spaces where they actually have the opportunity to question their gender, to explore who they are beyond what society or body parts tell them they are. It is a question that reminds me that folks like me are still needed to be able to help those searching—first to take a breath—and then recognize that there is no perfect trajectory for understanding identity. We all come to understanding of self at different times in our life. For many youth, they feel they need to have the answers *now* because their peers do, but that isn't how identity development works. More questions started to come out, I had found a connection with them all.

"Ryan, how do I know if my feelings are really about not being a girl, or just not wanting to be made to act like a lady?"

"Ryan . . . what do I do when my mom tells me I am such a guy because I didn't ask for details about an event?"

Suddenly voices started to topple on top of one another and I couldn't keep up. Everything shifted when a student, who had been silent for most of the meeting, enthusiastically yelled, "Gender is fake!"

The student was referring to how different societies and cultures create the norms around how people should act or behave based on being assigned male or female at birth. In a way, the student was right. Through the evolution of humans and different cultures, we have created social standards and norms around what clothes we should wear, if we should or shouldn't have body hair, what are appropriate lengths of hair, and how we should express body language. Where I still get caught up is how to recognize and validate social norms related to gender expression, while not invalidating a person's gender identity or linking it to being fake. Some people have asked me: "If we didn't put pressure around gender expression, and you could wear the clothes you want, and engage in the activities that you want, would you still have transitioned?"

"Absolutely" came out of my mouth before I could even form my thoughts. In college, I was already wearing the clothes that I wanted, and I was participating in the activities that I found interesting. My trans identity was not directly tied to my expression; it was tied to the fact that my body, not my clothes, was not a representation of me. This concept is hard for people who are not transgender to understand. It is also a place of frustration for people who are trying to understand the differences between their own gender identity and expression.

"Okay, everyone, our time is up, and we need to get Ryan to dinner before the event. Will we see everyone there tonight?" the trans man sitting next to me said while looking at his smartwatch. I smiled, we had the same watch, and the same propensity for keeping things on schedule.

"Yes" resounded from every voice in the room.

⚠

The topic of figuring out gender expression followed us into the auditorium that night. I stood up on a stage that could fit a full orchestra. Bright lights shone in my eyes, preventing me from being able to see the audience, only dark shadows that outlined heads and shoulders. The audience was an impressive size for such a small town, but over the years I've noticed that audiences are always larger in the rural or more conservative regions than they are in urban and progressive places. Among the shadows, I saw the outline of an arm pop up from the round heads. I pointed in the direction of the hand and asked, "Do you have a question?"

"How do you adjust to wearing the clothes that you want to wear, instead of what society expects you to wear?"

"Uh . . . by just not giving a fuck." I was a little shocked that I used the *F* word. Cussing is something I keep at a minimum when presenting, but after the conversation with the students today, I felt like it was needed.

The audience erupted in laughter. I was in the clear.

I followed my profanity by saying, "We are who we are. Individuality is what makes this world interesting and fun. Now, granted, my T-shirt and jean choices from prior to my transition to today are probably not that exciting, but I like them. They are my jam. Follow your jam." I have found that students like it when "old people" use their lingo, so I try to get a "jam" or "adulting" phrase into my talks to show that I am hip and in-the-know. This approach either does show I am hip, or it just makes me sound cheesy—either way, it gets laughs, so I just keep going with it.

After my talk ended, I zipped off the large stage and over to a corner where my book, *Second Son,* had been placed on a table for a book signing. A young child walked up to the table and peered at the cover of my book with a smile on their face. I could not assert if the child identified as male or female, but they looked to be eight or nine years old. I would learn later they were actually twelve. The child's dad stood there and watched me. He looked like your typical Midwestern dad, short and clean haircut, a round gut covered by a flannel shirt, which hung untucked over his Lee blue jeans. I could tell he was nervous as he picked up my book and read the back. He took his arm around his child's shoulder and moved over to the side so other folks could come up and either take a selfie, purchase a book, or do both. As the crowd started to dwindle, he set the book down and quietly asked if he could speak with me the next morning. I thought about the long drive home the next day, but decided taking a little time out of my schedule for him was important. We agreed to meet at the McDonald's in town at seven-thirty a.m.

As they both left the auditorium, a couple of the students from the support group came up to me. One of them was the student that had come to the group late. "I just wanted to come up and say hello, and say that hearing you several years ago changed my life." I instantly remembered that I had met her, before her transition, a few years prior at a speaking engagement. Seeing the changes, and hearing that my story had helped her, I felt propelled to wrap my arms around her shoulders and give her a big hug.

Over the years, I have picked up on the nonverbal cues signaling when a person wants a hug, but might be afraid to ask, for fear of being seen as creepy. I couldn't even keep track of the amount of times I have asked people, "Do you want a hug?" as they awkwardly sway back and forth between wanting to stay by me, but also wanting to leave. Whenever I ask, they let out a big sigh of relief and say, "Yes, that would be great." I feel like the hug gives them permission to go back out into the world while clutching their identity in their hands so that it doesn't slip below the surface and into hiding once more.

After letting my arms drop down from this hug, I took a step back and looked at her vibrant blue eyes. Her eyes and energy warmed my soul. It was the energy I needed from folks in the trans community to reassure me that I still belonged, that I was needed.

"I need to go to work, but it was really great to see you again. I loved your book, and am so sad that I lost it," she said, motioning down to the unpurchased copies left.

"Oh no!" I said. She started to turn around, but I shouted, "Wait! Let me sign a new copy for you."

"Really?! Thank you so much."

As I handed her a new copy, we made eye contact again and instantly went in for another long hug. Smiling, she turned to leave, following behind her was the student who sat quietly in the group that day. Quiet except for the one phrase that they decided to yell again in the empty auditorium, "Gender is fake!" Their voice echoed through the large room and followed both of their bodies out the door and into the cool spring air.

△

When my alarm clock went off at seven o'clock the next morning, I gathered my things and walked out to my car. I wasn't sure what was in store for me that morning, but I knew that me taking an extra hour out of my day might make all the difference for the dad and child I had met the night before. I walked into the McDonald's, the setup was like any other chain across the nation, making it feel familiar in an unfamiliar town. Scanning the booths and tables, I spotted the dad at a booth by himself. In front of him was a tray with one sandwich paper wrapping and another sandwich with a couple bites out of it. He was getting ready to take another bite as I walked up to him. He dropped his sandwich and slowly scooted his body out from the booth. I heard him grunt and could tell that his back was stiff, making me wonder how long he had been sitting there that morning.

"Good to see you," I said as I shook his hand.

"Thanks for coming," he quietly responded. I could tell he was nervous, both for meeting with me and possibly also being seen with me. He lived in a small town; word gets around in small towns. Having been raised in one, I totally understood everything going on inside his mind at that moment.

"Let me go grab something and I'll be right back," I said.

"Okay." He scooted back into the booth.

I returned with a burrito and coffee. I slid my tray onto the table before also scooting into the booth. In just two minutes, my back began to start aching. I knew that when I got up, I would also groan and put my hands on my lower back, just like he had done.

"Thanks again for coming," he partly whispered. "I know you probably have a busy schedule."

"Of course." I slowly started to unwrap the burrito, even though I wasn't hungry.

"I wanted to talk with you about . . ." He stopped speaking, and I could tell he was struggling with something. "Sorry."

"It's okay."

"I wanted to talk with you about my daughter, who was at your talk last night," his voice was soft, tears formed in his eyes.

I immediately felt ashamed for saying the *F* word with young ears in the room, but he didn't seem to mind.

"She keeps saying she is transgender . . . I worry that I've done something to cause this." He picked up his half-eaten sandwich and then set it back down, still holding back tears.

"No parent can cause their child to be transgender," I said, trying to reassure him. "Thank you for bringing your kid last night."

"I thought it would be good for her to hear you. I just worry. I want to support my kids . . ." Some more tears began to form in his eyes, proving even those that appear to be tough have the same emotions as anyone else. "I just . . . I don't . . . Religion is very important to me and I don't know how to love my kid, and support their decisions, when I know those decisions are going to make them go to hell."

My heart sank into my stomach. Religion is always the hardest thing for me to talk about because it is so dependent on individual beliefs. Even people who say they are Christians will have different beliefs depending on their denomination. As a person who is not religious, due to getting a degree in cultural anthropology, where I learned about all the different worldviews and creation stories, it's hard for me to find a way to connect with deeply religious folks. I looked down at my plastic tray, the ordered breakfast sat in its paper wrapper, turning colder and harder by the minute.

"I understand that religion is important to you, and recognize your worry around what happens after we die, but it is important to be able to support your kid while you are both alive," I said.

"In my teachings, changing your body is a sin. I know I can't keep my kid from doing what she wants to do as she gets older, but I don't know how to help her understand and live with her own sins." He pointed his index finger and put it firmly down on the table while leaning his head forward, like he was giving a passionate sermon.

My discomfort barometer was continuing to rise, even though I knew the person sitting in front of me was truly trying to figure out how to love and support his child, while also struggling with his religious beliefs. I looked into his eyes. I could see the turmoil he was experiencing and could only hope that something I said that day would help him, but going against the words "God" and "sin" made it a challenge.

"I don't want to invalidate your religious beliefs. As you know from my talk last night, organized religion is not something that guides my own life and my own choices. But as a person who is transgender, I can say that my life before my transition felt like living in some form of hell, compared to my life now. I am my authentic self, now that I've been able to transition. I would hope that you can find peace in knowing that if your child is transgender, the transition may be what saves their life and their relationship with you as they age." I liked to use "they," "them," and "their" pronouns when talking to a parent who was struggling, it was a way for me to respect their struggle while also respecting their kid.

The hour passed by at a medium pace, the heaviness of the topic and hardness of the seat didn't help move anything along. I felt empathy for the man sitting across from me. From my own experience with my parents, I knew how hard it was for them to come to terms with understanding my trans identity. Adding the religious piece on top of the trans piece can make it more difficult. Even with that difficulty, it fascinated me how hard religion can be for people who know deep down what the human thing to do is, the loving thing to do.

"I hope our time today has been helpful for you. I know this is hard, but supporting your kid is the most important thing, so I want to thank you for being open to exploring it."

"Yeah, thanks again for meeting with me," he said in a quiet voice. I watched as he dropped his head down, breaking our eye contact. I knew that when I left, he would most likely sit in that booth for another ten to fifteen minutes to process everything we had talked about, and begin to reckon with the torn emotions within himself. These are the most powerful moments when thinking about change; these are the moments where you recognize that beliefs may not align with reality and truths. The question he now needed to answer, without me in the room, is *Am I ready to love and trust my child, no matter how difficult the journey, or will my religious beliefs keep me from trusting the process?*

⚠

On my drive home, the familiar scenery passed by and below me, cornfields that were composed of piled dirt rows from the tillers preparing the soil for planting, and hilly roads creating the sensation of a roller coaster meant for very young children. Along the roadside, there was an occasional billboard erected in a farmer's field with the image of a baby next to the text *It's Not a Choice, It's a Baby*. A few miles from these signs were others that had pictures of what people in the United States imagine Jesus looks like: a bearded Caucasian guy with long hair, wearing a robe. Next to him was the text *Jesus, I Trust in You*. With the morning's conversation still repeating in my mind, I realized we live in a country that fears what we do not know, and so we need something to try and keep us grounded. It is scary, if you think about it. None of us truly know what is in store for us after we leave our physical bodies. How would people define the purpose of life if they knew after we die, there is nothing? After we die, we will not be reunited with family in a place full of fluffy clouds and happiness. What if, after we die, the earth just grows around us, or, more specifically, the bodies that we used to carry us. I don't have the answer to what happens after we die. However, having transformed my identity by living in two genders, and essentially two different bodies, I keep my faith and hope centered within my internal guidance that is led by my heart and instinct.

CHAPTER 2

EVERYDAY AWKWARD ASSUMPTIONS

Selfie 163 – November 2018

Is there a point in a transition where one reaches pure happiness?

It is a question that I am frequently asked by anxious individuals who are considering or who have already started their transition. It is a question asked by concerned family members and friends who want their child, sibling, or partner to finally feel peace within their body. It is a question asked by ambitious professionals who serve the transgender community, professionals who are seeking knowledge and those key points that will make them better providers. It is a question that I ask myself, and one that I still cannot concretely answer.

When a person first begins to think about transitioning, there are a thousand different questions, fears, uncertainties, and elations that roll through the body. As you come to the decision that you will officially be moving forward, there is a calm before another storm of emotions. Suddenly you pepper yourself with the questions: How am I going to tell people? Will they accept me? What will happen at my school or at my place of work? What name should I use? Am I ready to change my pronouns? What steps should I take first? Will providers work with me? How am I going to pay for this?!

In between the moments of sheer panic and joyful hope for the future, you just keep putting one foot ahead of the other, while researching everything possible about the physical transition and how people navigate the world in those beginning steps. While everyone's timeline is different, there typically comes a point in a transgender person's life where they are done with their "physical transition," and are able to walk through society living as the gender they wish they had been assigned at birth. We'd all like to think that when people reach this point, they feel whole, at peace, and satisfied with both their internal and external layers. We pin this hope onto the word "happiness," as if this emotion can drive out—and keep out—all the uncomfortable feelings that lie within us.

We are on that quest to achieve happiness, but how does it happen and how is it measured? Do you just wake up one morning and swing your feet out of bed, place them on the ground, and then say, "Wow, I am happy, I am content"? Is it brought to you after an amazing orgasm where you lay naked and sweaty next to your partner and have a warmth rush through your core and out to your limbs, numbing the pain and bringing forth the pleasure? Or is it that one moment where you are standing naked and looking at your reflection in the mirror, and you don't have the urge to either put on clothes or cover up with a towel and instead think, *Okay, I am happy . . .* ?

After completing several stages in my life where I think I have hit that point where I will finally be happy, I've had negative emotions—fear, anxiety, depression, or anger—pull me into their web. I am now learning that happiness cannot be measured by where people may be in their transition; in fact, the transition creates new conflicts that take a lot of insight to work through. While you now feel comfortable in your gender, there is a strange shift in how you are treated and seen within both the transgender community and society as a whole. Through my different experiences, I've discovered that people still do not see you, nor do they understand truly what you have been through and what you navigate with an identity now hidden behind the words "man" or "woman."

△

"I'd never know . . ." The drawn-out statement came from a seemingly impressed woman standing in front of me in an auditorium. I had just finished another talk about my transition and was getting ready to walk over to my book-signing table.

"You'd never know what?" I asked, even though I already knew what the rest of the line would be.

"If I hadn't heard your story, I'd never know that you were transgender." She continued to stand there, looking at my face while slowly moving her head from side to side, as if she were looking into a campfire. However, instead of being mesmerized by the different shapes and patterns of the flames, she was trying to get a glimpse at the wood underneath.

"Uh . . . thanks," I awkwardly replied.

Over the years, my feelings around hearing this statement have shifted. When I first started my transition, this comment would have been one of encouragement. To me, it signaled that I had officially moved out of that pubescent stage where sometimes I would "pass" as male, and other times people would stare a little longer to try and figure out my gender. Now, the "never know you were transgender" statement feels like a compliment rolled up into a backhand slap to the transgender community. It makes me wonder, *What do people think being transgender looks like?* Are we just supposed to stay stuck in that awkward adolescent stage of a transition so people can say, "Yep, that's a transgender person right there"?

"Just amazing," she said with a big smile on her face before turning around to exit the room. At least she didn't conclude with the common follow-up statement: "I just thought you were a gay guy!"

I let out a short snicker, my typical reaction to uncomfortable moments. I knew her comments were not intended to be an insult. However, I feel anytime we say something about a person's physical appearance, it can make the receiver of the statement feel more insecure. Even something as simple as "You look great!" can then make a person think, *What, did I not look good before?* For someone who is transgender, what makes comments about physical appearances even harder to take in is that it reinforces this feeling of people running a visual inventory of you, and then interacting with you based on those assumptions about your identity. How would she have treated me if she thought I was "just a gay guy"? How would she have felt about me if I had walked past her on the sidewalk and all she saw in that moment was a white man?

△

On the east side of St. Petersburg, Florida, a concrete wall has been created to shore up the land, protecting it from being pulled out into Tampa Bay. The wall is even with the grass that has been planted, allowing visitors to walk right up to the edge and gaze at the water five feet below. If you stand there long enough, you'll be able to see wild dolphins gracefully move through the shallow waters as they search for fish. I first discovered this spot when I was in St. Petersburg for an eating disorder conference. Since then, I have made a point to revisit whenever I am in the area for work. I feel tranquility when watching the dolphins' grayish-blue bodies come out of the water for a breath of air before going back under the green surface. In those moments, I am just a part of nature, a patient and respectful observer.

In the spring of 2014, I was back at my special spot watching the dolphins as the sun beat down on my skin, but this time I wasn't alone. To my left was a man who appeared to be in his late fifties, shirtless, holding a long stick and motioning different poses with his arms. It was as if he were preparing to go into battle with a large wooden baton. To my right were four teenage boys in swim trunks and goggles. One of the boys had a spear gun in his hand. I watched as he let out an excited scream before jumping into the water to shoot at whatever he felt he needed to destroy. I wanted to yell at them, but four large boys with a weapon versus one midsize guy just holding his cell phone didn't seem like a safe or fair bet if emotions escalated. The guy to my left let out a loud puff and made a motion that looked to signal the end of his workout. He then walked over to me while looking past my body toward the boys.

"They are being really stupid. That spear gun could hit one of the dolphins," he said before patting his sweaty brow with his T-shirt, which he had tucked into the waistband of his shorts.

"I know . . . I wish they would go away," I replied as the second boy laughed before jumping off the concrete wall and into the bay.

"My name is Damon." He extended a hand.

"Hi, I'm Ryan," I said while extending my own back to him.

"I was in Vietnam," he said while watching the boys. "Man, back then I was treated so badly because I am Latino."

"I'm sorry about that . . . Thank you for your service." This is a traditional comment I assume veterans appreciate, but also disdain because

16

thanking them will never heal what they experienced in war. For Damon, it would not take away the impact racism has had on him and his life.

"Where you from?" he asked.

"I'm from Nebraska."

"Nebraska!" He paused. "That's a red state . . . Boy, that isn't a good place to be a woman."

I could feel his heavy stare, which made me want to stop him and say, *"No shit, I know because I used to be one."* But I refrained.

"I'm guessing you're a Republican then. . . ," Damon continued.

"No!" I quickly replied. "I mean, no, I'm not Republican." Even though prior to age twenty-one, I used to be one. Growing up in a conservative farming town prior to the advancement of the Internet didn't allow much space for exploring politics.

"Okay, buddy. Well, have a good day." He made a point to pat me on the back before turning around and walking away, leaving me with the four rambunctious boys.

I wanted to stop him and yell, *"Wait! I worked for Planned Parenthood for over six years in Nebraska!"* But his back was turned, and I didn't really know what would be accomplished by this interjection. Instead, I just stood there, dumbfounded, thinking, *What just happend?*

⚠

While my encounter with Damon was *very* different, for some reason it had me flash back to a memory from when I was still a female-bodied college student in 2001. It was springtime and I had arranged a dinner date with one of my friends. I hated driving downtown because parking always stressed me out, so she had agreed to pick me up. I lived in a room in a three-story brick apartment building that was described as being "garden level." This was a fancy way to avoid pointing out that you actually lived in a room that was mostly underground, preventing you from being able to look out the tiny windows placed on the upper third section of the walls. Instead of staying inside my dark apartment, I decided to walk out to the curb, situated on a busy intersection, and wait.

As I stood there, I noticed a red sedan coming down the street at a slower pace than the other cars. The driver rolled down his tinted window and started looking at me, not the road. Instead of continuing forward on the street, he switched on his left turn signal and slowly drove down my block. In a few minutes, he was back on the other street, still driving slower than the other traffic before turning left to go down my block again. *That's odd,* I thought while hoping this time he would keep going west.

My hope faded away when I saw the red car appear on the other street one more time, but this time, after he turned left, he didn't drive down my block. Instead, he parked right in front of my apartment. I could feel my heart rate increase, but I kept looking in the other direction, hoping he was going inside to see someone. When I heard his car door close, and then footsteps come up from behind me, I knew he just wanted to talk to me. I cautiously looked over and caught a glimpse of him and his short stature out of my periphery. I watched as he took a sip of Coke, the red can glinted from the sun dropping near the horizon. He dropped the can back down to his side and ran his tongue over his teeth. His eyes were surveying me like I was a sandwich he was contemplating buying for lunch. I nodded at him, but then looked past him, hoping my friend would pull up soon.

"How much?" he asked in an African accent, before carelessly dropping the can to the ground. Not only was he being disrespectful to me, but he was also assaulting the earth, the place where I stood.

"Uh, I'm just waiting for my friend," I nervously replied.

He continued to stand there, looking at me, biting his lip while his eyes ran their fourth survey of my body. For the life of me, I could not figure out why he was standing there. I was not a feminine woman. My hair was never styled, makeup never donned my face, my body was hidden under a T-shirt four sizes too big for my frame, and jeans that looked more like big towels were wrapped around my legs. My body and being were the furthest thing from femininity one could imagine, but this guy somehow thought I was a sex worker.

"How much?" he asked again.

"I am just waiting for my friend," I restated. Fortunately, he gave up, turned around, and returned to his car, but not before making a sucking noise with his mouth.

I felt shivers run through me after he departed. This was not the first time I had an awkward and uncomfortable interaction with a man, but it was the first time someone had solicited me for sex. In these moments, you realize people see you differently than you see yourself.

⚠

When I first started my transition, I dreamed about the day where people would see me as the gender I identified with, but an interesting phenomenon happens when you reach that point. People have completely different assumptions about who you are, how they should treat you, and what they expect regarding how you will treat them back. My interaction with Damon was a new aha moment in my transition.

People outside my talks do not know I am transgender. They just see me as a bearded white guy. If we have a moment to exchange a few words, they will hear a feminine voice and may then assume I am a bearded white gay guy, but the one thing they feel they know for sure is that I am a white man.

Being a person raised with a minority identity, due to being female, then lesbian, and now transgender, I find it is a bit of a mind-fuck to be at a point when you can walk the world and be seen as a white man. Especially when you are fully aware that your appearance can be viewed as the problem with society, the face of racism, and the reason for sexism. The phrase "white-male privilege" is then pinned onto your shirt. To lump us into this broad term, it excludes and ignores the intersections of identities and everything that a trans man carries inside, and how he still may interact with people due to being raised female.

For me, this includes things like being aware of every step behind you at night when you walk alone or being told you don't deserve something because you weren't *pretty* or *pretty enough.* My experiences of being called a "dyke" and then a "fag" by strangers on the street, or being denied a job or access to health care because I am transgender, are hidden underneath what people choose to see.

Transitioning to male has not taken away these memories and interactions, but by looking at me now, people may more likely believe I am the perpetrator, not the perpetrated. Yet, the intention behind a transition is not to gain power and control over other people. Rather, it is to survive while searching for that feeling of being content. I've discovered that people have a hard time seeing below the surface in whatever the present state of the person standing in front of them is.

In my present state, I am seen as a white man. This is a description that in the social-justice sphere pisses a lot of people off. Feeling like you are now part of the problem in our society becomes even worse when people in the transgender community start to use your transition and appearance against you.

CHAPTER 3

ACCUSATIONS, APOLOGIES, AND SELF-AWARENESS

Selfie 139 – November 2016

You don't see a problem with a white, cis-passing, trans man speaking at a TDOR event? The harsh criticism, posing as a question, popped up in the comment section under an article titled "PFLAG honoring Transgender Day of Remembrance with guest speaker and diversity training." A professional photo of me was used as the placeholder.

By the time I discovered this comment, the day's schedule of events in southwest Missouri had ended. I had just returned to my hotel and opted for visiting the bar before retiring officially for the evening. Ordering a pint of beer had become my postevent drink of choice: *After all, I had worked hard and was emotionally drained, but was not ready to go to bed yet.* To keep me occupied while I sat on a bar stool alone, I would often go through social media to see if anyone had tagged me or wrote me a message. That night, I took my first sip of beer and then wiped away the foam from my mustache before pulling out my phone and opening up Facebook, where I saw that I had a new comment notification. Assuming it was someone who had attended the training that day, I clicked on the notification only to be greeted with, *You don't see a problem with a white, cis-passing, trans man speaking at a TDOR event?*

My thirst for beer dissolved and was replaced by a rock in my throat and gut. A "liked" icon popped up under the angry comment. The online world was receiving and outputting information before I had a chance to process the intent and motivation for the attack by a supposed "friend." I started to comb through the day, to identify what it was I could have done wrong.

△

I had been invited by the PFLAG of the Ozarks chapter to conduct training on transgender health care for local medical providers. Their monthly meeting for November happened to coincide with a day known as Transgender Day of Remembrance, or "TDOR" for short. TDOR was founded to memorialize the deaths of transgender people due to hatred and prejudice. In 1998, it began as a Web project called "Remembering Our Dead." It honored the unsolved murder of Rita Hester. Today, in-person events are spread across the world and are used to raise awareness around the senseless acts of violence that impact the transgender community.

I had gotten up early that morning to drive the six hours from Nebraska to southwest Missouri. I pulled into Springfield, a city that looked familiar, even though it was my first time there. Brick buildings—two to five stories high—sported large windows that showcased literature, art and antiques, bridal gowns, and real estate for sale in the region. As I drove down the two-way street, I saw people, predominantly Caucasian, walking past the windows and peering in before continuing their stroll, coffee cups in gloved hands. It was like many cities I had visited in regions with populations less than two hundred thousand in the Heartland. I followed my GPS to a small church located southeast of the city's main drag. I knew I was in the right spot after pulling into the parking lot and seeing two people carrying in materials with rainbows on them and bottles of water.

"Ryan, we are so excited to have you here!" I heard as I walked up to the entry. A woman, in her midfifties, stood in the doorway of a place where PFLAG members met once a month to support each other because they identified as LGBTQ or their family members did. As I got closer, she opened her arms, inviting me in for a hug. The brief warmth of both our bodies felt nice, since it was a blustery fall day.

"Thanks, Debbie. I'm honored to be here today," I said before releasing our embrace.

"If you remember, my husband and I first met you at the Philadelphia Trans Health Conference two years ago, and since then, we were trying to figure out how to get you here. We felt that the stars were aligned when we looked at our calendar and noticed that our monthly meeting landed on the same day as TDOR! Hopefully, we'll get more providers to attend because it *is* TDOR."

"I hope so, too," I replied while peeking inside to see what the setup would be like for the talk. Some churches have great sound and high-quality projectors; others have a portable speaker-microphone system, which cuts in and out, and a projector that can manage to get an image on the screen, but you may not be able to make out anything, even if it's there.

"Let's go in so you can get set up," she said while making an after-you gesture.

"Thanks." I walked in and continued my inventory of the room. I was pleased with the arrangements, minus feeling sorry for the attendees because they would be sitting on hard metal folding chairs for the next two hours. After injuring my back several years ago, I wouldn't last more than five minutes on one of those seats.

"Did you see the newspaper article they ran?!" Debbie excitedly asked.

"I did! In fact, I shared it on Facebook in case anyone in Springfield didn't know about the training."

Man, oh man, this would have been a moment where I wish I could have paused everything to peer into the future, to experience the feelings that would be evoked by one little post.

"I am so happy they did. It is hard for us to get coverage around LGBTQ issues here."

"I get it," I replied while having a flashback to one of my TDOR speaking events in Salina, Kansas, that received *a lot* of coverage in 2009.

⚠

Going into my line of work, I realized being an out transgender man who speaks to audiences in both rural and urban settings would invite the opportunity for people to treat me poorly. I had my first newsworthy taste in 2009 when the Westboro Baptist Church decided to protest a talk I was giving at an off-branch of Kansas State University in Salina, Kansas. It happened after the university initially declined having me speak on campus due to it being close to Thanksgiving; they feared that the topic would not be of interest among their student body.

In 2009, talking about transgender identities was considered even more controversial than it is today. The *Salina Journal* (the town's local newspaper) wrote an article with the headline COLLEGE NIXES TRANSGENDER SPEAKER. This article quickly hit the AP Newswire, leading to coverage across the nation and up into Canada. Infuriated by the news, students on campus created a petition. Along with the unexpected coverage, the students' voices and signatures on the petition won the battle. The "no" turned into a "yes" and I was scheduled to speak on their campus, three days before their Thanksgiving break.

The news also made its way to the Westboro Baptist Church, which quickly weighed in by inaccurately writing all about me on their blog. They took it a step further by having some of their members travel through the small city of Salina with their large, horrendously bright yellow, orange, and green neon-colored signs on the day I was scheduled to speak. Up to that point, in all of my years as a speaker, I'd never asked for security.

That night, I was assigned to a security officer, who escorted me to the event and had me enter the building through a back door. I never saw the angry protesters; I also never saw the 150 counterprotesters that stood on the other side of the street. The Westboro Baptist Church members, which numbered a pathetic four, stood alone, tucked into their street corner. Rain started to pour down, smearing the hateful words written on their posters. The counterprotesters shouted out words of love, diminishing the clan's energy to shout out derogatory and offensive phrases.

Along with their love, the counterprotesters held a fund-raiser known as a "pledge-a-picket," meaning however long the church's clan stood out in the rain, people could pledge money. After a half hour, the quartet left, ugly signs in tow. During that half hour, the fund-raiser brought in over a thousand dollars, which was donated to the Matthew Shepard Foundation. The Shepard charity was founded in 1998 after Dennis and Judy Shepard lost their son, Matthew, who was gay, to a violent hate crime in Laramie, Wyoming.

The organizers had me wait to enter the room I would be speaking in until they had everyone seated. After announcing my name, I opened a large metal door and walked into a room of roughly three hundred people in attendance. There weren't enough chairs for all the people that wanted to hear me speak, so many stood in the back, while others went to an overflow room where they could watch me on a television. The final outcome of the event was a positive experience for me and for the community, but I knew that hostility driven by assumptions from the online world would only increase in the future.

△

When I discovered that the Springfield paper had written an article about the training I would be providing on TDOR 2016, I was fearful that protesters could congregate at the church, like they had done in Kansas. Fortunately, the forty people that entered the church and ended up occupying the hard metal seats were there to learn, not to pass judgment. I opened up the talk by covering the differences between gender identity, gender expression, and sexual orientation; then I dived into the different intersections that impact someone who identifies as transgender within the political, societal, familial, and medical landscapes. I always felt good when a training ended and I knew that health care providers would leave with a little more information about how to work with transgender patients, especially when these providers were located in less populous areas.

"Thank you so much for the training and for working with me to get everything I needed for continuing education hours," Debbie said after the talk.

"You're very welcome," I replied as I packed up my computer and other materials.

"Ryan?" I heard a different woman's voice say my name, prompting me to look up from the bag that I was packing. In front of me was a face I hadn't seen in well over fifteen years.

"Mrs. English?" I said in disbelief while looking at my eleventh-grade English teacher. Yes, the irony that her last name is English, and she taught English, was one we all teased her about as teenagers. She smiled and nodded her head up and down, happy to have surprised me.

"What are you doing here?" I exclaimed.

"I moved down here a few years ago and now teach at the university," she replied. "I was looking through the paper this morning and saw that you would be here, so I wanted to show up and give you a hug." She opened up her arms and I leaned down and gave her a long squeeze. I always felt validated when people who were teachers and mentors from my past showed up to support me, especially after I had transitioned. While hugging her, I realized I hug a lot. I don't recall being a huge hugger prior, but that has changed since my transition. It's partly due to me being more comfortable in my body, so I feel more comfortable having bodily contact with another person, but also because I feel like we are all wanting more in-person connection to keep us feeling grounded and safe.

Debbie was still standing there, looking at us with a mixture of confusion and curiosity contorting her face.

"Debbie, this is my high-school English teacher!"

"That is so great! Thank you for coming," Debbie said as she extended her arm for a handshake. "We were just getting ready to take Ryan to the TDOR event at the GLO Center, which is the longest-running LGBT center in the city! Would you like to join us?"

"That would be great!" Mrs. English said while looking up at me.

"That sounds great to me, too. Thank you for joining us," I said while putting my arm around her shoulder. Looking down at her, I wondered what emotions were going through her body. Not only had she been one of the people who taught me how to write, she also served as my drama and speech coach in high school. I wondered what thoughts were going through her mind as she stood next to me now, seeing my transition, my speaking, and my book *Second Son*. She was someone who had influenced me. I hoped that she recognized it with pride that day.

⚠

The emotions in the room during TDOR are a perplexing mixture of somberness and fear that collides with empowerment. This event was no different. I stood in the corner of a room that could fit fifty people comfortably, but there were at least sixty-five there that night. Two women walked into the center of the space, slowly prompting the excited crowd's buzz to dwindle into a calm murmur. The group's silencing was guided by a lingering shush. One of the women walked up to the microphone with a piece of paper in her hand. The other stood by a table draped with a black tablecloth held in place by several rows of candles. In her hand, she held a candle lighter, hovering near the wick closest to her.

"Thank you all for coming tonight," the first woman's voice came through the microphone. She continued to speak to the importance of TDOR and the history of the LGBT center. Everyone's eyes remained glued on her as she began reading from her piece of paper. "Monica Loera," she read, then paused. "Jasmine Sierra. Kayden Clarke. Maya Young . . ." With each name that was read, the woman at the table would light another candle.

In 2016, considered then to be the deadliest year for transgender people, there were twenty-seven candles to light. Each flame represented a life we lost to murder. Each year, the majority of the names, and the candles lit for them, belonged to transgender women of color, killed by a boyfriend, acquaintance, stranger, or a person in law enforcement. These were victims not only from violence but of the big four: racism, sexism, homophobia, and transphobia. The speakers concluded with the victims' names and asked for a moment of silence.

I bowed my head down and closed my eyes. Images of the victims ran through my mind as I thought about what life would be like for people if they were loved and accepted by their family for being LGBTQ. Can you imagine if we all were loved and accepted by society no matter our sexual orientation, gender identity, or color of skin?

This was my eleventh TDOR event, and while many things have changed for the transgender community since 2005, the number of people murdered, assaulted, or harassed continues to grow. Sadly, the United States has the third highest murder rate of transgender people worldwide, falling behind Brazil and Mexico. After the TDOR event, I was taken back to the church, where I provided a two-hour talk about my own transition and experiences living in the Heartland. At times, it can feel defeating, but it's also motivating to continue to share stories with the hope of building more support through visibility and education.

It was approaching nine o'clock by the time I got back to my hotel. When I saw the comment online, I became completely deflated. After spending the day focused on raising awareness for people attacked because they are transgender, I had a different form of attack coming straight at me. I had learned over the years not to have knee-jerk reactions to things posted online. In fact, I usually automatically delete an offensive comment and block the user, but by looking at this person's tiny profile picture, I could only assume he was a young trans man. I decided to keep his post up for the evening as a placeholder to return to after I had time to process my own thoughts.

I paid my bar tab before going back to my hotel room to try to get some sleep. That was a pointless endeavor. The whole night, I tossed and turned as I felt my heart rate increase with anger toward this person. My anger would then begin to simmer with the increase of time between my heart's beats. In these quieter moments, my internal, doubting voice told me, *"Ryan, you are not wanted and should never speak again."* I gave up lying in bed when the alarm clock hit five-thirty a.m. I let out a big exhale before swinging my legs out of the bed and gathering my things for the drive home. I figured a six-hour drive would be a good time to try and further process the words used, and why they bothered me so much.

I was all too familiar with the ever-changing landscape around language and gender, but the word "cis-passing" was a new one for me. The word "cisgender" is used to define a person whose sex assigned at birth and gender identity are aligned. Scientifically, the word "cis" means *on this side of* and is the opposite of the word "trans" which means *across from*. Though it was first added to the Oxford Dictionary in 2015, the academic community started in 2010 to slowly adopt using the term "cisgender" in order to delineate from someone who is "transgender." To say that a transgender person is "cis-passing" is to suggest that they are no longer oppressed because they can walk through the world without having someone know they are trans.

For a trans person to write this on my wall, they erased my lived experiences. They shunned my identity and all the work I had done since day one of my transition to raise awareness for the community as a whole. They also assumed I do not experience, nor have the potential to experience, victimization. Yet, because I am so out and public about my identity, that thought sits in the back of my mind every day. Since becoming a public figure, I've received death threats and weekly threats of violence toward me through all different online platforms. These threats cause me more anxiety when I am on location for a talk, or when I am walking through a community where my speaking engagement has been advertised. When you have undercover police officers sitting in your audience, others standing in the doorways, and two assigned to escort you on a college campus, it makes you pause for a moment and think, *Wow, they are worried someone is going to shoot me.*

When I was female, I had a visible minority identity. With my transition, my marginalized identity is now hidden underneath my exterior appearance. It is not a visible target, like skin color is in our country. I fully recognize that I have more opportunities and privileges afforded to me simply because I was born in America as a Caucasian. Over the years, after I have undergone all the different challenges, barriers, hoops and loops, to transition, I have a male physique and bearing. Yes, on the surface when I walk into a room, I have white-male privilege. But to judge another person's lived experiences solely based on what you see on the surface, well, that is doing exactly what trans people and other minority individuals do not want done to themselves.

I began to look past the words this person had used and thought about what they might have been asking. I inferred that deep down what he was trying to ask is, why would a trans person who can walk this world seen as a white man speak at a memorial event where the largest number of people who are victims are transgender women of color? First, I was not speaking at the TDOR event, but even if I had, the question I would pose back would be: Can't white trans men (no matter where they are in a transition) also be victims of violence, lose someone to violence, or be impacted through other forms of victimization because they are also part of this marginalized group?

Let's be honest, the fact that we even have TDOR sucks. The fact that transgender women of color are disproportionately impacted is heartbreaking and infuriating. These memorial events should absolutely be a space where transgender women's voices shine to raise visibility and to get us to think more about how to counteract racism. I am fully on board with white people continuing to evaluate how we can use our privilege to work alongside and raise up those who are oppressed. If me no longer being a professional speaker with specific specialties would end this injustice, I would step down in an instant and put my life's energy to something different. However, my life's work is dedicated to helping break down barriers for transgender and LGBTQ people of all identities.

I've worked long and hard to build a career and to craft presentations that get people to stop, think, and then move forward with action. In all of the places I've traveled, I have not seen how this culture of "othering" transgender people based on a hierarchy of perceived privileges helps break down the barriers and increase support for the community. It just makes people scared of offending one another, so we keep fracturing and splitting to the point where there are no voices left that feel empowered to speak. As an end result, it leads us to disengage from the community and the ways we can contribute to the cause.

While driving, I kept trying to craft how I could write that as a reply without it blowing up into an online tornado of career-ending destruction. My SUV slowly went back and forth from the right lane to the left, passing the other drivers that did not have their cruise control set to exactly five miles over the speed limit. My phone was clipped into my air vent, Google navigation was up and running on the screen. An alert notification popped up across the top, my so-called "friend" had just posted another comment on my page. I usually do not click on screens other than my navigation while driving, but I had to know what he said. A lump formed in my throat as I saw another comment underneath the article about my training.

I'll say it again, you don't see a problem with a white, cis-passing trans man speaking at a TDOR event? My approach of allowing myself more space to process how to reply respectfully had apparently backfired. It appeared that not responding had made him angrier. I started to feel sick to my stomach and yearned for the open landscape in front of me to be cut open like a movie screen. I envisioned driving my car through it and off this set created by other people's projections instead of reality.

After crossing the Missouri state line and entering into the southeast corner of Nebraska, butting up against Iowa, I felt heaviness take over my limbs. In that tiny corner sits Richardson County, where Brandon Teena had first been raped and then murdered. The energy in this region is negative and nauseating. I wanted the online attacker to be in the car with me so that I could talk to him about my personal experiences and what I've witnessed over the past fifteen years being transgender in this country. I wanted to talk to him about regional privilege and how the Heartland is quite different from Los Angeles (where this person lived). It is a region where being transgender and queer is not protected or accepted at the state level. It doesn't matter what a person sees regarding first impressions. Once the transgender or queer identity is revealed, the risk and fear of being harmed, fired, or denied health care turns into a reality.

Two hours later, I was back in Omaha, pulling my car into the detached garage and shutting the steel door to close me off from the outside world. I walked into the kitchen through the back door, where my two long-haired dachshunds were eagerly waiting to greet me. I squatted down so that they could perch their front paws on my knees before the three of us nuzzled our faces together. I had always been more attached to animals than people. I knew I could trust them. I stood back up and let out a big sigh. My phone buzzed with another notification; I feared it was him again, and I was right. This time, though, he didn't post on my regular page. Instead, he went to my fan page, where the article had also been shared. *SINCE YOU DIDN'T ANSWER MY QUESTION ON YOUR OTHER PAGE, I'LL POST IT HERE. You don't see a problem with a white, cis-passing trans man speaking at a TDOR event?*

This was getting out of hand and I really hate it when people use all caps in a message, so I decided it was time to block him and delete his posts. I didn't want this to be perceived as a power play, but his hostility and disrespectful tone made him lose having access to me. I do not interact or engage with bullies, especially when that bully is typing their hate. As the online world continues to grow, we see that real-life assaults often begin as a vaguely ominous posting on social media. I can't even count the number of times people have left comments threatening to hurt me, kill me, or just wishing I would die. The dire possibility for potential bodily harm spurred by an angry comment sits at the back of my mind and propels me to tread very lightly online.

Pushing fear of violence aside, the more time I've had with social media, I've learned that if you look underneath the surface and not form judgments based on a headline, you learn a lot more about who a person is and what their intentions are. The online world, however, doesn't have time for deeper-thought processes. It is driven by individual opinions, along with the anger that keeps the person behind the keyboard in a defensive place. On top of the anger, society has created this belief that if you send or post something online, you should have a response within milliseconds. This desire for immediacy hinders the opportunity for processing feelings, exploring the language that was used, and crafting a thoughtful response.

⚠

Two days later, I received another notification alert. Someone had sent me a private message. I found the message in the often forgotten "other" folder—a folder where messages from people who are not on my "friends" list are housed. I clicked on the message; it was from my online attacker. I took in a big gulp of air and then slowly exhaled before reading the paragraph in front of me.

It's just I thought you were a role model for our community— which means I thought you were someone who wanted to be the best person they could be—which also means I thought calling you out on your privilege would be a conversation. His message continued by noting that he was not apologizing, but simply wanted to acknowledge how his question could have come off as accusatory. He closed by stating that he assumed I would have been open to the question.

I considered not writing him back. His acknowledging that his "question" was actually an accusatory statement, but then refusing to apologize for his approach, sent a message of entitlement to me. However, I feared not responding would make this person become even more hostile toward me, my name, and the work that I do. So I did what people socially reared "female" do, I wrote a heartfelt apology to this person.

Why am I apologizing?! Especially because after I sent my apologetic response, I received another message. This time, it came from one of his cisgender female friends who informed me of my privilege and how terrible it was for me to delete the other person's post. She went on to inform me that the person identified as a trans masculine, nonbinary person of color. These were identities I was unaware of, since I couldn't surmise or assume anything from a tiny thumbnail image, but it didn't matter to me. His lack of civility and rudeness was what stood out. I wanted to respond to the friend, but she made it so that I could not reply, an action I likened to taking a dump in a person's house and not flushing.

I stood there and shook my head. This is the world we live in now, tossing out weighted words and labels as a form of power, a way to silence voices and erase the identities we don't want to accept or feel should not be seen.

Since I am perceived as a role model, even after receiving the second accusatory message from his friend, I decided to engage in an e-mail conversation over the course of the next few weeks. Sadly, I do not feel anything was resolved on either end. He was steadfast in his views around what he felt would end disenfranchisement by attaching my face to being a white male, instead of being a transgender person. Mind you, a transgender person who was trying to be the best person he can be! I've learned, though, that being the best person you can be *cannot* equal perfect or elicit approval from everyone in the world. Plus, what one person may define as "the best person you can be" will look different to the next. After being put up on a pedestal, and struggling to stay within its narrow boundaries, you are eventually going to fall off what the viewer has placed you upon.

⚠

Unfortunately, after this experience, the call-out culture and the idea that attacking our own will end injustice have both continued to grow online. I started hearing more people say that white trans men who appear to fit within the binary should *not* use their voices. They should remain silent in order to lift up the voices of people who are *more* oppressed. I can appreciate people's compassion around exploring how to end individual and interpersonal forms of oppression, in order to chip away at systemic oppression overall. However, pointing fingers and labeling one another based on assumptions, or what we see on the surface, keeps us stuck in the same oppressive place we are trying to claw out of.

I personally feel deflated when I hear someone refer to a trans man as being "binary." This is a misguided and highly assumptive statement that pushes a trans man into the hyper-masculinity box that the observer has formed. If you were to look at a picture of me, I do look more masculine. If you were to engage in a conversation with me, you would see I am a blend of both masculinity and femininity, as most of us are.

Telling a trans man to remain silent just reinforces the messaging we are all too familiar with from our prior identities: being told to be quiet and stand in the background. We would frequently hear this commentary when we were viewed as female and perceived as not having recognizable power or self-worth. Now we are being told to remain silent and stand in the background *after* our transition. This time, it's because we are men and supposedly have privilege. Feeling like we have nothing to offer to help create change, we then respond with the all-too-familiar words:

"I'm sorry."

"So sorry."

"Am I in your way?"

"Am I taking up too much space?"

"Here, let me move a little farther out of the way."

"I should be quiet?"

"Okay, I'm so, so sorry for speaking."

What I then internalize is that in order to raise up others, I must erase my own existence. It can feel really defeating at times, especially when you've worked hard to create a home in your body, but the outside world still insists that your home is not the right address.

CHAPTER 4

THE SOUR PATCH OF BEING EYE CANDY

Selfie 96 – May 2013

White orbs lingered in my vision with each flash of the bulb. "Great, now stand up a little taller and pull your shoulders back," my friend Fred instructed me as he moved around the small room, camera in hand.

I followed his directions and puffed out my chest knowing that with each click, Fred was capturing different contours of my shirtless body. Fred had first started photographing me in 2007, and with each year that has passed in my transition, he has documented both my physical changes and my changes in self-esteem. I felt insecure the first time I took my shirt off in front of him. It was one thing to have my buddies, who were also trans men, snap the monthly pictures of me in a poorly lit room with my little Canon PowerShot camera. It was quite a different thing to be standing in front of a black sheet, which had been pinned up to the wall, and behind bright lights on either side of me. Meanwhile, a professional photographer used his very expensive camera to capture not only my body in high resolution, but also every pore in my skin.

"Awesome, now . . . give me a hard stare." The camera clicked several more times as I hardened my jawline and gave the camera a "smize" (a word we can thank Tyra Banks for) with my eyes. Shooting shirtless photos can be fun and feel liberating, but we had scheduled this particular shoot to capture images that I could share online to celebrate my transition's eight-year anniversary.

Many people celebrate anniversary dates in their transition by posting photos. It is a way to provide encouragement to others, and a way for us to look back over the years and be in awe of our own physical transition. For people on the trans masculine spectrum, chest surgery is one of the most freeing surgeries to undergo. No more sports bras, no more binders, no more hiding underneath big sweatshirts, even when it is ninety degrees out. Chest surgery not only frees us from these physical barriers, it frees us from the anxiety that clouds our mind because of what is on our chests. To celebrate this freedom, we share pictures of our results, the healing process, and the changes that come with the passage of time.

"Okay, I think I got it," Fred said while looking down at the screen on his camera. A grin formed on his face, pleased by what he had just captured with one click.

"Great!" I exclaimed before running over to my T-shirt, which I had draped over his office chair. For me, it was one thing to be shirtless for a photo, a shower, or a plunge into the ocean, but I was always quick to put a shirt back on after those purposes were over. I am not sure if my discomfort around being shirtless was because of my body image issues, or all the messaging I had received and perceived growing up around women needing to cover up and not reveal too much. Perhaps it was both.

"When is your anniversary again?" Fred asked as he walked over to his desk to plug the SD memory card from his camera into the computer. Photos of me in different clothing, poses, and shading started to pop up as thumbnail images, row by row, on his monitor.

"Next week . . . year eight!" I peered over his shoulder, my smile turned to a grimace when I saw a few shirtless photos pop up that didn't look too flattering due to a goofy look on my face or an odd twist of the body.

"Great, I should be able to get some of these back to you by then," he said while reaching over for a pack of cigarettes. After smizing for the camera, I felt like I also needed a smoke, but knew I wouldn't be joining him outside in a few minutes.

"Thanks, Fred. I always appreciate you doing this for me." I looked down at him and grinned. I was lucky to have him in my life. He had become my digital historian, documenting monumental life moments—moments that have become my badges of honor and celebrations of manhood.

I posted my anniversary photos for 2013 and added the caption: *My 8 years on T torso documentation. Going on 34 and still seeing changes.* Likes quickly started to pop up under the image, along with comments and questions. I patted myself on the back because I was doing what I thought people wanted from me, showing my trans body to provide inspiration and support.

A week later, an anonymous letter arrived in my mailbox. When I unfolded the piece of paper from the unknown sender, I was greeted with one paragraph, typed. It referenced the photo I had posted: *Stop, for all of us, just stop, okay?*

I dropped the letter to the ground.

Trans men find connection through showing chests that have different ranges of battle scars. As we age, testosterone transforms our bodies, and our scars begin to fade. This causes our trans identity to slowly tuck underneath our skin. When we post shirtless photos after we are no longer "visibly trans," people quickly try to lead us back to where we had been prior to surgery by telling us to cover up. The more your scars can't be seen, the more likely you will be labeled a narcissist for showing your chest in a shirtless picture. Additionally, it's more likely someone will call you out for being insensitive because you were able to access something (in this case chest surgery) that other people can't. It is a weird double standard, even weirder when you keep flip-flopping on either side of it.

Being transgender, you quickly see how messaging around gender deeply impacts our understanding of self and expression, and also how quickly society can push you into the box it feels most comfortable with constructing. What we need to understand is that a given label and the associated box do not define a person, but rather confine them. It is one of the reasons why photo documentation of my transition is important to me. It takes me and others through points A, B, C, and D. It makes people pause and begin to question the labels, boxes, assumptions, and judgments they have formed about me and about themselves based on our appearances in our present states. I am saddened by how short-term our views of one another can be, and how quickly we find new language to use to devalue one another.

△

In 2005, I joined a few other brave trans men by deciding to launch a public website that would document my transition. At that time, social media wasn't prominently used, and hashtags were still just a pound symbol, so there weren't many resources out there for people who were thinking about transitioning, or who needed guidance during their own transition process. When I was a child, I had a diary where I wrote all my private thoughts before locking everything away with a key (a pointless gesture since you could easily unlock it with a paper clip). When I was an adult, my diary became a webpage, a transition diary that wasn't kept inside a box underneath my bed. Instead, every week I shared with the online world the changes I had experienced due to testosterone, recovery from a surgery, or how I navigated the legal process in a time where being transgender was still something "you just saw on TV."

We needed visibility. We needed a feeling of connection to pull us up from being consumed by fear and hopelessness. Transition documentation websites put a face to an identity, a face that was more relatable than words. Along with these websites, we also found information or support by joining Yahoo! chat groups. In these groups, our faces were thumbnail-sized avatars and we had usernames like "Harry02331."

After 2008, my website and its three years of content started to get put on the back burner. Social media platforms were slowly becoming the go-to places for resources. I tested the waters by joining MySpace and quickly discovered that I loved being able to post pictures, write blogs, and also pick three songs that would play when people visited my profile. I didn't even take offense that my "friend" Tom never visited. MySpace allowed me to start interacting with other trans people that went beyond user names like "Harry02331." Sadly, just as our community started to build up on this platform, we all started to jump ship to the new shiny object, Facebook.

Suddenly it felt like our lives were shifting from being inside an enclosed and safe room to being inside a glass house. Gone were the avatars with anonymous names; in were places where we could see a person's full name, birthday, occupation, and pictures we posted or were tagged in. When signing up, we all agreed to terms and conditions that we've now learned give away all of our data.

The way social media is designed, we have lost our privacy and ability to have a shield for protection. We all now sit in front of our small or large glowing screens; faces defined by the shadows drawn along the ridges of our features. Disengaged with those physically around us, we press our thumbs against the screens and run them up and down like we are playing slots with an endless supply of credits. Our interactions and emotions are now shared through a thumbs-up, heart, or an emoji that laughs, looks surprised, cries, or fumes.

Needless to say, I am not a fan of what social media has become or how it shapes our opinions of one another. I would love to run away from it all and delete every online account. But, with the growth of business taking place via online interactions, I have come to believe that my livelihood depends on those accounts: validation over irrelevancy, keep up or be phased out. The online world now constantly lurks over my right shoulder and waits for when I have insecure moments to pull me in.

You have no purpose, I think while staring at a calendar with blank date after blank date.

Should I be posting something on social media? My anxiety continues to rise as I ask myself if I am relevant or worthless.

Why did that person unfollow me? I decide I am irrelevant and worthless.

Am I posting too much? I fear people will label me a "narcissist."

Am I posting too little? I believe people have labeled me "out of touch."

If I don't get my numbers up, people won't value me as a speaker. I see my life's work crashing to a halt.

What hashtag should I use? I want to slam my head against the wall because I hate that relevancy relies on the pound symbol linked to a word.

What used to be fun for me, a hobby, was quickly turning into something I hated. What used to be a place of comfort, a place of support (for the most part), a place to find connection, felt like it was transforming into a shark tank laced with chum, each of us taking opportunistic bites. The bites have noticeably increased with the shift on how we use social media, and how we value others on the different platforms. When we started to place value and worth on how many followers a person had, the popularity contests that used to be held within the confines of our middle schools' and high schools' walls spilled out onto the walls of the online world, which consumes our individuality.

△

The social media shark tank moved from a lackadaisical swirling tornado to a full-on feeding frenzy the day the "Top Ten List of Hot Men Who Were Born Women" started to pop up online. Due to all the visibility I had provided over the years, and Fred's great photo-taking skills, my name and an image of me shirtless, smizing at the camera, were included. I was flattered . . . at first. While many people refer to me as being attractive, the voice and feelings I had as an insecure adolescent and young adult, which led to my eating disorder, continue to propel negative and critical thoughts surrounding my appearance as a man. My confidence quickly turned to insecurities when more websites began to publish varying versions of these lists with exploitative titles: "Look at this! Did *he* used to be a *she*? Click to find out!"

Websites knew these types of lists were sensational clickbait, so they were popping up on site after site. The headlines, photos, and captions incited people's anger at the men who were listed, even though we had never been asked to be part of these lists.

When the lists were posted on social media either by guys listed, or by people that tagged us, the platforms that once helped us to connect became the places where we were pitted against each other because of how the media depicted us. People started to smear one another online, made nasty comments about how other trans men looked, and critiqued the worth or value of us as humans.

Great, another depiction of a heteronormative trans man who is reinforcing the binary.

Ugh, these guys just have cute privilege.

I can think of twenty other men that deserve to be on this list instead of these guys.

And the complaints continued.

A terrible outcome from all of these criticisms is that they pinned the blame on the guys in the photos, not on the media franchises that published our faces and names (again without our permission). An even more terrible part about the guys getting attacked is that these were all folks that had put themselves out there—some for over two decades, some for over a decade, and some who were newer to the scene, but were still creating dialogue and giving people hope. We cannot control the fact that mainstream media pushes us into the same box we were in prior to our transition, plucking whatever image from Google they feel will get the most clicks. Our bodies and identities continue to be sexualized and objectified, with the added bonus of being sensationalized because we are trans.

I feel pulled by both ends on this awareness. On one hand, it is extremely affirming to be able to feel comfort in your body and be able to show yourself with confidence. There is a reason why nudity is so prominent throughout history. Nudity strips us down to our most vulnerable places, but also our most empowered places. Think about as children, right out of a bath, how we would streak through a room, flashing our booties for all to see. While on vacation in Mexico, I saw a family with three-year-old twin daughters who were bathing buck-ass naked in the outdoor shower by the beach, with not a care in the world. As a person with what was a severe eating disorder, and who still has a debilitating negative body image, it has been freeing for me to be able to have a photo taken of my body, and not feel completely uncomfortable looking at it, or having other people see it and me.

On the other hand, the attention we receive purely because of our bodies, mostly very well-defined masculine bodies postsurgery, puts us as trans men back to what we experienced when we were female-bodied. We only get attention because of how we look, not who we are as a whole person, what our professional knowledge or skills are, or how we give back to our communities. With these images, we also see only one spectrum of trans men, one that ignores men without surgery, men without muscles, men with bodies that are different. We remain seen as sexual objects, while all other parts of our identities are invisible, including our voices.

After several attacks from people I had helped in the past, as well as complete strangers that just wanted to be jerks, I began telling myself that our world is on information overload. I maintained that no one would miss my feelings or experiences. Thoughts of suicide crept back into my mind as my internal, negative voice told me, *"You are of no value."* I first struggled with suicide ideation at age seven when I realized my body was female, not male. As a female college student, I struggled because I didn't have a place where I fit in with anything: my body, community, or family. As an adult man, I struggle because of the bullying and judgment that happens online or the dismissive words said under people's breath that eventually travel back to me through one channel or another.

In my field of work, we often talk about the drastically high rates of suicide and suicide attempts in the transgender community. A national climate survey on transgender health, conducted by the National Center for Transgender Equality, reports that **40 percent** of the participants have attempted suicide at least once in their lives. For me, it has been twice. When we talk about suicide risk and prevention, we point toward the importance of having supportive families, affirming communities, and access to transition-related care. Many people who have experienced suicide ideation talk about how their decision not to move forward was made by having just one supportive person in their life.

If we can't find support in the community where we live, it helps to find support among other transgender people. This is why I plead for the transgender community to end contention toward one another. Without acceptance, we can't find a place of comfort or a group of people where we feel like they inherently understand our struggles without us having to explain them. Again I ask you: What would this world look like if we could just be kind to one another? How different would it be if we recognized that life has challenges for all of us, no matter what privileges (real or perceived) we might have?

Since I am a sensitive person, hurtful words had a way to wriggle into my brain and form phrases that I began to believe. To try and ground myself after going into these dark places, I began to think about some of the people who inspired me in my own identity formation. For many in younger generations, you mention these people's names and they look at you blankly. To them, I am mentioning a stranger, a person who has had no influence in their lives. Yet, these were the people who inspired me and helped me find my voice, which has now inspired others. I get scared by the fact that within five years—and even now—when my name gets mentioned within circles of trans men, there are many blank faces. This fear fuels the belief that we are all bleeps. Here one day, gone another.

Some people may argue that even that bleep is important, as it is part of putting life around us in motion. We move, and then others move: pure physics.

I knew that I needed to start to shift my energy and focus in order to keep myself from feeling like I was vanishing from a photograph, a cause, and then from this world. I also had to start addressing my feelings around the attacks I had experienced online; they were starting to find their way through the cracks in my thin armor and beginning to break my spirit. I told myself that the flying arrows and flung spears would not end, mainly because many people like to bring down the folks they think are capturing or dominating the attention they want. As a result, I needed to start reframing my view of social media.

I hovered my mouse over the blue sign-in button and took a deep breath to prepare myself for entering into what had become a traumatic space. After clicking the button, I started to scroll through my followers and friends. Thumbnail images of smiling faces from diverse people started to fill my screen. These photos reminded me of my beautiful connections—no matter our age, race, ethnicity, body size and abilities, sexual orientation, gender identity, political affiliation, religious beliefs, or nationality. We were supporting one another and checking in on each other's individual journey; we were moving past labels and embracing the whole person. I realized I had been focusing on the negative, not the positive, and it was quickly pulling me underneath the water. I needed to swim back to the surface. To do this, I needed to get offline and reach out toward the relationships that were tangible and standing right in front of me, the relationships that got me to where I am today.

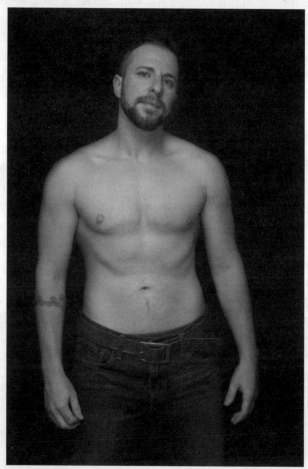

Photo by Fred Schneider

PART TWO

A WEDDING AND FOUR FUNERALS:
STORIES OF LOVE, CONNECTION, AND LOSS

*"This is the pits." Her blue eyes did not blink as she said this;
rather, they stayed locked on my face.*
To this day, her words "this is the pits" both haunt and amuse me.
She had just summed up life.
*A part of us wants to keep going, but eventually we realize we
need to get off this ride.*

—Ryan K. Sallans

PART TWO

CHAPTER 5

LOVE MAKES ME A BETTER MAN

Selfie 64 – August 2010

"I'm going to marry that woman." These six little words slipped out of my mouth so seamlessly that one would think I had already thought this through, but I hadn't. As my proclamation about my girlfriend, Lily, spilled out over the rugged landscape of the Rocky Mountains, I found myself surprised and questioning if I should try and pull the words back in. Also surprised was the man sitting across from me. A man whom I had just met three days ago during our road trip to Colorado. As he looked at me, warning signs with CREEPER, FAST MOVER, or HOLY FUCK were most likely blinking over my head, since I had only been dating Lily for one week.

For any of us who have fallen in love, we quickly realize that rationality often gets thrown out the window. This was something I had to remind my concerned friends and family who, after my transition, always saw me as rational and responsible Ryan. I shopped the clearance racks at the department stores so that I could buy what everyone else was buying, but for almost half the costs (the downside to this was being a season behind with the latest fashion, but again it was half the cost). I lectured people about never letting their gas tanks go below half a tank; I mean, what if the gas tank was on empty and there were no gas stations in sight? I would go to bed around nine or nine-thirty at night so that I wouldn't be too tired for the six o'clock alarm clock. I also have never received a speeding ticket, thanks to setting my cruise control so that I never go more than five miles over the posted speed limit.

So, not surprisingly, the day I announced that I was leaving my longtime partner, Michelle, to begin a new relationship with Lily, mass chaos erupted among those close to me, who questioned my sanity. Their well-intentioned freak-outs turned into widespread panic when they saw me start to buy clothes that were not from Target, at full price, and still in season! Or when they saw me jump into my car at eleven o'clock at night to drive the hour distance to Lily's house for a sleepover. As I drove, my odometer would start to inch up to ninety miles per hour in a seventy-five-miles-per-hour speed zone, all while I belted out show tunes from the first season of *Glee*. I'm pretty sure that if my friends had known about the show tunes, they would have most definitely pulled me in for an intervention.

I was literally a different person, a person that did a one-eighty within a forty-eight-hour time span. My friends labeled me as manic and questioned if I was in a sane state-of-mind to be making any big life decisions. When confronted, I could only say, "Don't worry about it. I'm in love!" The love bubble had been formed and could not be penetrated by any person's concerns. The moments where you can freely and guiltlessly sit with the person you are falling in love with are moments that pass by, but, in lucky situations, have a lasting impact. I was confident that I had finally met the right match for me in Lily. Her intelligence, professional drive, mysterious beauty, and overt social awkwardness were all qualities that kept me wanting to wrap my arms around her, but also stand in front of her to clear the path, even though she didn't need any help.

⚠

Three days into dating, and me admiring everything new that I learned about her, she asked, "Do you want to go to Colorado with me over Labor Day weekend?" This was not only going to be a getaway into the mountains, but also a trip to see her family.

I felt nervous about the idea of going on the trip. We had just started dating and would be staying at her ex-stepmom's house before traveling up to spend a couple days with her dad. Still, I didn't think twice before saying, "Yes."

Fortunately, Lily invited two of her friends, who were also a couple, Brian and Jeremiah. Although I didn't know them, the buffer they could potentially create between me and Lily's family was very appealing and helped to lessen my anxiety.

The car ride to the mountains was going to be over eleven hours, so another tradition Lily had was leaving by four-thirty in the morning in order to have time that first day at her ex-stepmom's house. While I was a morning person, four-thirty was not a time that generally registered to me as "morning." It still felt like "time I should be sleeping."

Needless to say, the alarm clock was obnoxious that morning; the fact that it was still dark out was even more annoying. As we waited to get picked up by Brian and Jeremiah, I shuffled through my duffel bag of clothes that had been traveling the last week with me to each place I crashed since leaving what had been Michelle's and my home. With each place I slept, the clothes in my bag became more and more entangled with one another. Usually, I would just grab whatever matched, but this morning I wanted my tightest black shirt and nicest jeans that accentuated the small curves of my butt. Finding the right clothes was a bit rough at four-thirty in the morning, especially since I was operating on three to four hours of sleep each night, but I managed. I had never wanted my body to be seen by a person the way I wanted Lily to see me. If Brian and Jeremiah happened to sneak a peek at me, I was also okay with that. It felt good to finally have people comment about my appearance in a positive way.

The long trip was great for Lily and me, but in looking back, I imagine it was pretty painful for our traveling companions. I acknowledge that we were the annoying new couple in love that giggled at everything the other person said. We participated in PDA, even though we weren't aware of it, and longingly looked at each other, believing these feelings would never ever end. When we reached our destination, I could tell the guys just wanted a glass of wine and a moment without our sighs and long-held glances.

As I stepped outside of the car, my lungs were greeted by the Rocky Mountains' cool and clean air. I took several breaths in, taking in the smell of sage and river water. It was a stark contrast to the Glade plug-ins in Lily's house. We were in a neighborhood that was nestled in the valley; with every step I took, all I saw was red rock smattered with green. Even though I had never been there before, I felt like my spirit had just returned home. After grabbing our bags from the trunk of the car, we walked up to the front door. Before we could knock, it swung open. Standing in the doorway was a petite woman with shoulder-length red hair, clear blue eyes, pale-white skin, and a smile running from ear to ear.

"Y'all made it!" Her voice held a Southern twang. "You must be Ryan. I've heard a lot about you. My name is Elizabeth," she said as she bypassed the handshake and went straight for a hug. It was not a half squeeze, with a light-pat-on-the-back hug, but a full-on squeeze.

"Hi! Yes, I am. I've heard a lot about you, too," I said while in her embrace.

"You know, Lily was telling me about you several months ago, and I just *knew* you two were going to be together." She stepped back to look at both Lily and me. Her lips were pressed together and formed an approving smile. I looked over at Lily, who acted cool, not acknowledging the fact she had been talking about me way before we announced our love for one another. Her profession as a therapist had allowed her to master the calm face, even if someone was sharing something unexpected.

"It is so nice to have y'all here. Let's go set all of your bags down and then just relax. Just make yourself at home."

We moved past the threshold and I was blown away by the high-vaulted ceilings composed of large wood beams setting on top of drywall. A fireplace, encased in stone that went from the floor up to the twenty-foot ceilings, was the only thing separating the family room from the dining room. Past the dining room were large glass doors that opened up to a patio and terraced flower garden. Standing at the top of the garden, before the mountain range extended into the sky, was a large wood structure with wood slats crisscrossing each other to create shade without an umbrella. I would later learn that this was a "pergola." Fancy words like that were not taught to me as I grew up in Nebraska's farmland.

"Wow," I exhaled. Even though I was running on very little sleep, my eyes were completely wide open, taking everything in.

"It's beautiful, isn't it," Lily said.

I looked toward her and nodded my head. I truly was in a fairy tale. Behind us, I heard the clinking of glasses and turned to see a bottle of wine and a cheese platter set out on the patio table. I had never been a wine drinker, but Lily and I had agreed that she would try beer and I would try wine. I also rarely ate cheese. When I did, I considered "good" cheese to be the cheapest stuff you could find in the discount grocery store aisle. Looking at the spread, I realized I had a lot to learn about fine-dining culture. I snatched up a cracker smeared with skunky blue cheese and settled into the fluffy cushions that sat on top of the wrought-iron chairs.

After everyone got a couple sips of wine and crackers in their stomachs, chatty conversation started to swirl around and in between us. At this time, I was careful about revealing too much about me, my work, and my past. I wanted everyone to get to know me as Ryan before they learned about my transgender identity. My silence around my identity became harder to control when Brian brought up transgender people and various aspects of transitioning.

The educator in me wanted to take over the conversation and correct the misinformation, but I wasn't ready yet for everyone to turn to me with the look of *How do you know so much about this topic?* So I remained quiet by stuffing my face with cheese, crackers, and sipping . . . okay . . . gulping wine. Fortunately, Lily specialized in working with transgender people, so she was able to correct information that was too far off-base.

The next morning, I learned an important lesson: My Irish blood was meant to drink beer, not wine. This is a lesson that I would continue to learn as the years passed, but I kept flunking the exam. Shaking off my mild hangover with a shower and coffee, I gave myself a pep talk before heading out the door to meet Lily's dad, Mike, who was divorced from Elizabeth and lived in a town forty-five minutes up the mountain.

When he opened the door, I saw a man about the same height as me. He had similar, angular facial features to Lily's, but his chin and jaw were hidden by a gray-stubble beard. Lily had warned me on the way up that her dad was more politically conservative, but he was very welcoming to her lesbian and gay friends. Since he didn't know about my trans identity, I made sure to give him a solid and firm handshake, and to stance myself as a guy's guy. This is not easy for me to do. It felt like a form of drag, since I am not the type of guy that spits, scratches, or uses the phrase "You got it, buddy" on a daily basis.

I was waiting for him to look sternly at me and say, "So you are the new boyfriend . . . what are your intentions with my daughter," leaving me sweating and saying, "Well, sir, I plan to court your daughter and later marry her, sir." Instead, he simply said "hello" and "nice to meet you" before moving on to what hike we were all wanting to do that day. Knowing he was an avid hiker, I was confident that we would be able to find some common ground and form a bond.

Before we began, I looked at Mike to assess what type of hiker he would be. While his body was in good shape, having just a touch of a stomach, he was also almost thirty years older than me, so I worried about him being too slow. When we reached the trailhead, Mike took the lead and I fell into line directly behind him. Some hikes start out with a flat trail that gradually increases in elevation; this hike started out with a steep incline, which never stopped.

As we started up the trail, I learned pretty quickly that Mike was a really freaking fast hiker. I was a fast walker, but when there are rocks and elevation involved, I tend to slow the pace just a touch. Mike's light feet bounced up the rocks like they were on springs. To keep up, I had to push out any concern for safety or fear of tripping on a rock and falling. The others took their time going up the mountain's path, but I kept my feet moving fast as I scrambled on the loose rocks. I desperately wanted to slow my pace so that I could first catch my breath; the high altitude made it feel like I was breathing through a straw. But I also wanted to take in the scenery around me, instead of just glimpses of Mike's ass as I looked up the trail to see how close I was to him.

"Well, here's the spot," Mike said in his hippie voice. Even though he wasn't a hippie, he just sounded like a guy who had been to every Grateful Dead concert since the 1960s.

We came to a stop. I slurped up the air, while finally being able to look around me.

"Wow." We were standing in a valley at the base of, according to Mike, "the most photographed mountain peaks in the nation," the Maroon Bells. In front of us was a lake that reflected everything surrounding the bowl where we stood. The ominous-looking peaks were softened by fluffy clouds, which inched by; sprigs of green, which you could see descending the mountain, became thicker with each hundred-feet drop in elevation.

Mike's voice interrupted my moment. "Well, uh, I guess we should find a spot to sit down while we wait for the other three."

I looked over at him. He had removed his sweat-soaked ball cap and was running a handkerchief over the top of his head. I noticed, then, that he was bald on top, but had hair on his sides. This reminded me that some form of major hair loss was something I had to look forward to as I aged, due to the testosterone I was injecting and my genetics. I followed him to a shady spot underneath one of the Alpine trees and plopped down next to him. At that moment, I realized my goal of keeping up with him also put me in the position to have to be alone with him. I looked back down the trail; there was no sign yet of the rest of my pack. *What do I say to the guy who is my very new girlfriend's dad? Not just her dad, but a guy who has no clue I am transgender. . . ?*

"So tell me more about this area," I said. Success, I knew that the safest conversation to have when in uncomfortable spaces was talking about the weather, unless the subject of climate change came up. Being in the wilderness and learning some of its history was also a safe topic, unless we started to dive into land rights and colonization.

"Oh, well, uh—" Mike started to talk about the area, but was cut off by Lily's voice.

"Hey!" she said as she walked up to us. Brian and Jeremiah were another twenty feet behind her. They all looked relaxed and only slightly sweaty. I was now off the hook, and able to take a backseat in the conversation and interactions.

As we hiked back down the trail, I realized that portraying myself as a guy's guy was not needed, nor was it authentic. Several months later, when Lily disclosed that I was transgender to Mike, he still welcomed me with open arms.

When we returned to Elizabeth's house that night, I began to feel more and more certain that Lily and I were right for each other. When looking at our work, we already knew we fit; seeing that we also clicked when it came to family, friends, and recreation, I just knew we were meant to live our lives together.

△

These realizations take us to the moment, the next evening, when I firmly said, "I'm going to marry that woman."

It happened while I sat under the pergola at Elizabeth's house. I was looking down the rocky path onto the patio where Lily stood. She was holding an orange flower, which she had just plucked from the garden. She started to run the soft petals over her long fingers, always needing to touch the different textures in front of her. We had just returned from another hike, so she was still wearing her hiking shoes, khaki shorts, and a light black jacket. A pink-and-tan bandanna covered her hair. Large sunglasses covered her eyes. She looked mysterious, her angular features half hidden, half revealed. I was still adjusting to the fact that she was my girlfriend. I was also still adjusting to being able to look at her, study her, and not be seen as the creepy guy who always stares.

The sun was starting to set behind the Colorado mountain range, only moments were left of the warming sun's rays touching my skin. I was in a deep trance when the words "I'm going to marry that woman" came unconsciously out of my lips.

This trance was broken by Jeremiah's surprised voice to my right.

"Reealll ... llyy ..."

While his drawn-out affirmation of what I just said hung between us, I felt my cheeks flush and sweat bead on my skin. I slowly made myself look toward him, only to see a smirk, proud to have some of the hottest gossip of the trip. His glass of wine remained tilted toward his face, a lit cigarette perched forgotten in his other hand. Blame it on the booze and the mountain air; blame it on the euphoric high I had been on for the past week. Blame it on whatever you want, but I didn't regret my oversharing. I was indeed going to marry that woman.

Someday.

I could tell he wanted to share the gossip with Brian, and every one of their friends back home. However, being the only non-vegetarians on the trip, we had established our own bro code, which I had hoped cemented trust and sworn secrecy.

⚠

The day came for us to return home. Lily and I crammed our long bodies into the backseat of the red Honda and settled in for the ride.

From time to time, she would lay her head on my lap and I would begin to stroke her hair. I looked down at her and studied the path my fingers took as I ran them along the outline of her ear. Being close to all of her, and taking it in, I started to feel like the man I had always dreamed I would be. In this position, I felt like the protector, the guardian in our relationship. This was important to me, since I had just left a relationship where the person witnessed my body and identity transform from female to male, from lesbian to an orientation still undefined. Lily had only known me and my body as male, as Ryan. I no longer felt guilty or apologetic about who I was, and beyond the internalized dysphoria about the size of my penis and the curvature of my hips, I no longer felt *as* ashamed about how my body looked.

⚠

The next year, during the same weekend, on the same day that I pronounced I was going to marry Lily, we were back in Colorado. It was nearing five o'clock at night, the same time a year ago that I foretold my own future. Lily was standing in the kitchen, slicing tomatoes for a Caprese salad. Before meeting Lily, I had never tried a salad that consisted of basil, tomatoes, mozzarella cheese, and balsamic vinegar. I loved how she had expanded my food box.

I watched as she laid the tomato slices carefully next to the mozzarella; her long fingers then carefully placed basil leaves on top. I zoomed in and studied her left ring finger, before looking at the rest of her hand. No jewelry currently encircled any of her fingers. She actually hated jewelry, but I had hoped that in a few minutes she would make one exception. In the pocket of my khaki cargo shorts was a hammered titanium ring, with a small black diamond set in the metal. I had had it made by a local jeweler in Omaha, where we lived. Over the past year, we had casual conversations about marriage and about what type of rings Lily liked. She didn't know that I held on to every word she said and took mental notes about what would be appropriate.

"Hey, babe," I said.

"Uh-huh," she responded softly as she focused on the salad she was making.

"How about you put everything down for a second so that we can go outside and watch the sun set."

"Okay . . . just give me a couple minutes."

I looked down at my watch. I wanted to propose at the same time I had my revelation the year before. "The salad can wait, the sun can't."

"Okay, fine," she said. She set everything down and dried her hands on a dish towel that had an image of a cat on it—her ex-stepmom loved cats.

As we headed out the door, I reached my hand out for hers and we walked up the stone steps to where the pergola stood. We both looked around and sighed. It was another gorgeous night on the western range of the Colorado Rocky Mountains. As she was looking to the side, I studied her profile. Perched on top of her small nose were her large sunglasses. Surrounding her glasses was her olive-toned skin, with a few sun spots starting to show due to her belief that her Italian skin didn't need sunscreen.

We had been together a year. During this time, we had gone through some hardships. Certain difficulties were things that any couple could go through, like the financial strain when I resigned from my full-time job—with a guaranteed paycheck, health insurance, and 401k—to become a full-time speaker. Other hardships were directly related to Lily being partnered with a trans man, including the stress of finding health care providers that knew how to address my health needs. When I had a health concern around one of my testicular implants, which had been placed two years prior, we hopped on a plane to Belgrade, Serbia. I needed to have my surgeon conduct a revision because I didn't trust any other surgeon to do it. We had weathered the changes and struggles together. I knew it was time.

"Last year, in this very spot, I sat with Jeremiah while looking down at you on the patio. You were holding a flower and looking out over the garden. While it had only been a week, I blurted out, 'I'm going to marry that woman.' Today I am in the same spot, at the same time, asking you if you'll marry me." At that moment, I got down on one knee and pulled the ring out from my side pocket. While I figured Lily knew about this all along, she actually had no clue.

She started to cry and said, "Yes, of course, I'll marry you."

I placed the ring on her finger, relieved that I had it sized right.

I stood back up and we kissed. Her arms were wrapped around my neck and squeezing me tightly into her lips, while my arms were wrapped around her waist squeezing her tightly into my body. In that moment, anything beyond just being in love disappeared.

CHAPTER 6

FINDING PEACE WITH BEING A PET DAD

Selfie 77 – September 2011

My eyes burned; the salt seared through my membranes more quickly and more aggressively than I remembered from my childhood. People say that we become less tolerant of pain as we age, but at thirty-three, I didn't think I should be *this* less tolerant. I took my wet hands and rubbed both eyelids, hoping it would help ease the stinging sensation, but it only made it worse. My hands were wet with the same salty water that had just hit me dead-on from the unpredictable waves of the Atlantic Ocean.

I hadn't been body surfing since I was eighteen. I hadn't been in an ocean, at all, for the past fifteen years. The way the waves pushed me around—lifted me up and tumbled me down—made me feel small but mighty at the same time. I was on the tumble setting of the washing machine and loving the youthful bliss that ran through me with each shift in the water's pattern.

Lily, now my fiancée of three weeks, had pulled me out into the ocean at five o'clock that night. She was the one that made me forget, or at least ease up, on my adult brain's rationale of a shark's prime feeding time being between five to seven at night, which increases a person's risk of being attacked. (I lived in a landlocked state, but learned this helpful factoid from Shark Week on the Discovery Channel.) Being out in the waves with her and hearing her laughter, I was reminded of what living is supposed to be about. It isn't about fear. It isn't about the most rational approach. And it certainly isn't always about me evaluating my transgender identity.

Suddenly being in the ocean during a shark's prime feeding time turned into just fun. Time, dates, age, body parts being seen by others, identity, names—nothing else mattered. We were having fun, and without using time as a reference, we stayed out in the water until the chills started to permeate our skin and harden our joints.

"Race you to the beach!" Lily yelled as her lanky arms started a windmill motion and her long legs started to kick through the water.

I ignored the fact that she had just gotten a head start, and I also didn't let gender dictate who should or shouldn't win the race. I began to charge my stockier build ahead of her, memories of my teenage years and the hours upon hours I would spend swimming, racing friends in a lap pool, or seeing who could hold their breath the longest, rushed past me in sync with the water.

"Beat you!" I yelled with my camera-caught finish. I rapidly shook my head back and forth to kick off the water dripping from my hair so that it wouldn't drip down into my eyes.

"No fair. You're stronger," she replied as she gently slicked her dark locks back behind her ears. Her svelte five-foot-eleven frame joined my five-foot-ten frame and we began to stomp up the shore transitioning from the compact surface to the loose sand hitching a ride on our wet feet.

I reached out my hand, and hers quickly shot forward to join us together. It was one of those moments where I would joke with her, "If this were a movie, the screen would go blank and show us moments later in a passionate embrace." This would be one of the movie scenes recorded in my mind as a reminder that we have a kismet connection. It was unlike the other movie scenes that would fade out, only to then show a coffee mug being flung across the room, or duct tape down the center of the bed. I knew those moments would happen, too, but I tried to keep the gushy ones more prominent in my mind.

"Thank you for making me come out tonight," I said.

"I didn't make you do anything, but I'm happy you joined me. I was coming out here with or without you tonight!" She reached her finger out and jabbed me in my side.

We had spent the past week in Atlanta, shut up in a hotel for an international conference on transgender health care. From Atlanta, we boarded another flight that took us to a beach house in Charleston, South Carolina, as a little getaway. It was a trip that wouldn't have been possible without Elizabeth's invitation, and one we dearly needed. While Elizabeth was excited to show us around the city she grew up in, we were excited to swim in the ocean and scour the beaches for the perfect seashells.

Lily and I both worked tirelessly in the transgender field and have found that our work, combined with my transgender identity, makes us forget that there are things outside of being transgender. Being on that beach, shirtless with only my swim trunks set low on my hips, and not thinking about my scars or what people think of me, is another moment I try to take an internal snapshot of. I want to store it away as a reminder that I am more than a transgender man. I am a human who wants what other people want: healthy relationships, laughter, and relaxation.

I let go of her hand and grabbed both of our beach towels. Like a maître d' setting a dinner table, I floated the towels over the sand until they were positioned parallel to each other running east to west.

"Thank you, honey."

"You're welcome," I replied as we both sprawled on our adjoining towels and looked out toward the endless horizon.

The sound of the seagulls, mixed with the waves beating the shoreline, made me feel as if we were listening to Lily's sound machine. This time, though, I felt serenity from the natural recording, not irritation from the manufactured sound bite that I wanted to throw out the window.

I leaned back, using one of my elbows as support, and crossed my now-hairy legs and started to watch the little kids splashing in the waves. I was always amazed at how much longer they could stay in the water without feeling cold, but then again, I have heard that the smaller the surface area, the more compact and warm things are. Parents and other adults scattered the beach. They sat in their beach chairs with their magazines and coolers nearby, and I began to wonder if Lily and I would be like that if we could have children.

△

It was a thought that brought me back to my transgender identity. Up until that moment, I just felt like a guy with his gal enjoying the beach, like any other couple. Then the thought of having kids, and the reminder that we couldn't have a biological child or an "oops" baby, snapped me back to the reminder that I'm not just "a guy."

My peacefulness turned into sorrow. This was the second time in my life that I experienced grief when thinking about not having genetic children. The first time this happened was in 2006 after I learned that my hysterectomy had been pre-certified by my insurance company. The days leading up to my surgery I struggled with a sense of loss because I knew that after completing the procedure, my eggs would be gone, and I would never be able to pass on my genetics and pieces of myself to another human being. This grief subsided during my recovery. I had found that the mental and physical relief of having those parts out of my body outweighed holding on to the eggs for future children. From that point moving forward, I decided I was content with being a pet dad to fur babies.

Having this second sense of loss wash over me as I observed the other people's children playing in the rowdy waves took me by surprise. I looked over to Lily and began to study her face. My imagination then slowly started to assemble what I thought a child would look like if our genes were combined. It made me sad to think that we would never be a couple that could talk about this beyond just curiosity. We would never make official comments like, "I hope they get your nose and my ears."

⚠

"What are you thinking?" Lily asked, pulling me back.

"Huh?" I looked over toward her. Her hair was beginning to change from sleek and smooth to curls with frizz. "Oh . . . nothing."

"Come on, tell me."

I looked out toward the kids on the beach. Some were bent over, searching for seashells; others were frantically digging for the creatures that had just spit out water through holes in the sand. "I was just wondering what it would be like to have kids and how we would be as parents."

"Do you want kids?" she asked.

"The funny thing is, no, I don't . . . but I wish we at least had the option."

"I get it. It makes me sad, too, but you know if we wanted a kid, we do have options."

"I know. I just wish we had the easiest one."

After saying this, I realized how ridiculous it sounded. I knew plenty of couples that have penises and vulvas, complete with sperm and eggs, that still can't get pregnant, or they go through countless fertility appointments to make it happen. It isn't necessarily the "easiest one." I then realized that this time, my envy wasn't about the kids and it wasn't about passing on my genetics. This time, it was about the fact that I didn't have a big penis and that I didn't have sperm. It was about the fact that I didn't have something someone else did, and it made me feel foolish and selfish. I felt like the British kid in *Charlie and the Chocolate Factory* who said, "But, Daddy, he has a squirrel that cracks nuts. I want a nut-cracking squirrel."

"Sorry, I sound stupid," I mumbled.

"I'm not going to lie. It would be nice to have the choice, but it is also nice not having to worry about getting pregnant."

"Kind of a dichotomy, huh?"

"It is. . . ," she replied as she reached over to push my bangs out of my face. My hair had also shifted from being sleek to frizz and curls.

I looked over and smiled at her. I then leaned over and gave her a small peck on the lips. We both leaned back. Our gazes locked onto each other, simultaneously, propelling us back toward one another for a deeper kiss. With our stomachs beginning to grumble and goose bumps prickling our arms and legs, we knew it was time to head back up to the house for the evening. I let her take the lead and found myself placing my slightly larger bare feet inside her footprints imprinted in the sand.

The connection between where Lily had been and where I was going electrified the bottom of my feet and sent shivers through my limbs. *I am connected with something beautiful and someone who will continue to challenge me.* I knew I needed to remember this when I felt the distance between us.

CHAPTER 7

LAW AND DISORDER

Selfie 79 – November 2011

The flashing of red and blue made the room I sat in turn into a purple hue. The colors made me feel dizzy, and I could feel my body sliding off the stool I was attempting to sit on. I leaned against the high-top table to stabilize myself. As my hands grasped the table's wood planks, I looked over to Lily, who was sitting to my right. Her face looked drawn and extremely thin, making her sharp features even more prominent. I could see the tendons in her long neck tightening with each swallow. Her small shoulders shrank into herself, like she was trying to disappear. I turned away from her and looked across the table; a police officer was sitting on the other side. The meeting we were having was not my or Lily's first, and it wouldn't be our last. We hadn't broken the law. We were filing another police report.

⚠

Earlier that morning, I had just parked at the grocery store and was starting to open the car door when I felt a buzz. I dropped my hand from the door's handle and pulled my phone out from my front jean pocket. An image of Lily, smiling while standing in the mountains, was on my screen. It was rare for her to call me during a time that wasn't at the top of the hour. As a therapist, she worked in blocked-hour time frames with each patient, so I would usually get a two-minute call from her when one patient had left the couch, and another was waiting to be invited into her office. I quickly pressed on my screen to answer her call.

"Ry . . . Ry . . . Ryan." She had trouble getting her words out. Her voice was frantic and high-pitched. I was instantly concerned. I wasn't greeted by "Hey!" or "Hi, sweetie"; she had said my name.

"What happened?" I asked. My heart went into my gut; my gut went into my throat.

"A letter came in the mail at my office."

"Okay . . ."

"It was addressed to you . . ."

The color in my face went from a pink-and-peach hue to pure white. Having a letter addressed to me, but sent to Lily's office, was another disconcerting incident to add to a rampantly growing list over the past year. It began two months into our relationship. I had just landed in Wisconsin for a speaking engagement when I received the first frantic phone call from Lily. She had just received a voice mail where a woman told her that she was concerned about her spouse, who had been following Lily individually and also us as a couple. Lily's fingers stumbled with her phone as she punched in the numbers to call the person back. Her body shook with shock as the person's voice began to list the color of our house, where our bedroom was situated, and what time at night Lily turned off the bedroom light.

When Lily shared everything with me over the phone, I felt completely helpless. It was one of the downsides of my job. I couldn't just cancel my event and hop on a flight home, even though all I wanted to do at that moment was swoop her into my arms and hold her forever. The next day, Lily called the police and requested that they come to her office so that she could file a report. No action, though, was taken against the caller's spouse. Shortly after we learned that we were being followed, we received an odd holiday greeting card that lacked a return address. When we opened it up, all it said was *hugs and kisses to Ryan* and was signed by two names we did not recognize. Due to the nature of Lily's work as a therapist, this card freaked us out; a large number of her patients were transgender, so we chose to keep our relationship extremely private. With me being a public figure that many of her patients knew, we were trying to figure out how to navigate setting boundaries and avoiding people's assumptions.

A year later, we were still not very public, only our close friends and family knew about our relationship. This letter was more evidence to what we had already feared from the voice mail, phone conversation, odd letters, and online threats. Someone had been, and was still, stalking us.

"What does it say?" I asked.

"I think you just need to come here. I canceled the rest of my morning."

"Okay. I'll be there in ten minutes." I quickly closed my car door, abandoning my grocery list and shopping trip. My heart pace quickened to the point that it was hard for me to take in a breath. My vision began to blur, making the lines on the road and the cars to the side and in front of me indiscernible. Lily's office was located downtown in a building called the Flat Iron, like the one in New York. Nestled between a fork in the road, the building had a curved front with sides jutting out at forty-five-degree angles, making it look like a triangle sitting on its side. It sat in a lonely area in the downtown, an area where the majority of the buildings surrounding the Flat Iron were vacant. Their only inhabitants were tiny rodents scuttling around in the layers of dust. Minus the rodents, Lily's office building was starting to join the others; only a few tenants resided within the walls of the four stories. It felt like a ghost town, which was appropriate for a building with several testimonies of ghost activity, including a man wearing a top hat, who was called Charlie by the tenants.

When I arrived, I bolted up the four flights of stairs, swung around the corner, and sprinted down the long hallway, where a large wood door stood, closed. As I turned the gold doorknob to enter, my body's motion came to an abrupt stop. She had locked the door. I knew she was fearful for her own safety every day that she sat in her office. I gently knocked the "shave and a haircut" tune so that she knew it was me. My breath was heavy as I sucked in oxygen, which I had forgotten to breathe during my sprint. I heard the door click and watched the knob turn. As the door swung inward, I could start to make out her frame. While her right hand held the door, her left arm was wrapped around her, tucking the sweater she was wearing closer and tighter to her thin body. I lunged forward to give her a hug. Both of our hearts were beating from our chest to the point that we could have joined them into one showstopping pound.

"Let me see it," I said as we released one another.

"It's over on my desk." She led me through her waiting room and into her office. A business-sized envelope sat on her desk; next to it were several pieces of paper. I looked at the envelope first. There was no return address, but my name was typed above Lily's office mailing address. I set it back on the table and picked up the letter. It was typed, and there was no signature at the end. The words hazily joined together as I felt both anger and fear filling my chest cavity. The anonymous author was demeaning my body and emasculating my identity.

"Call the police," I said.

It didn't take more than twenty minutes for a police officer to arrive at the door. Even though the police station was literally across the street from Lily's office, he drove his police cruiser to the building and parked it outside, lights flashing. The colors bounced and climbed up the brick and stone walls of the surrounding buildings. Two knocks echoed through the waiting room, summoning me to the office door. A face that was young and fresh came into frame. It felt surreal, like I was watching a cop drama from the front row of a movie theater. His left hand rested on his belt, while his right hung to his side. He stood my height, and his blue uniform was ironed and was trim-fitting on his body. *He must be new to the force,* I thought as I escorted him over to the high-top table that sat next to a coffeemaker in Lily's large waiting room.

"Tell me what happened," he said. The tone of his voice was calm, and his demeanor was nonthreatening—a characteristic I didn't think I would see in someone who worked for law enforcement. The sight of a police officer usually made me nervous, invoking a rush of questions through my mind. *Did I pay for my items? Was I driving recklessly? Do they know I am trans?*

"A letter came to my office addressed to Ryan," Lily said.

"Where's the letter?" he asked. Lily stood up and walked into her office to grab it. When she came out, she was shaking.

"Let me make a copy of it for you," she said before heading over to her printer.

The officer looked at me; in two minutes, he would be reading a letter that attacked my transgender identity. Lily and I knew that when filing the report, we would have to disclose that I was trans, which made us both anxious. We didn't know how an officer would treat me as an individual, or us as a couple, but it was a detail we couldn't leave out. Lily walked out with the copy in one hand and the original in the other. She began to extend the letter to place in front of him. I watched, nervous for what would come next.

"So, just so you don't get confused by what you are reading . . . I am transgender, and from what we've read in this letter, and what we have received over the past year, we know someone is stalking us," I said. I was happy to see that he didn't flinch when I disclosed my identity. I knew that far too often transgender people were not treated well when interacting with law enforcement.

When Brandon Teena went to the police department to report that he had been raped, which is extremely difficult for anyone to do, the police officer treated him like the criminal. The officers demeaned him because he was transgender. A week later, Brandon was murdered. For many victims, it feels like law enforcement is not designed to protect them, especially when those victims are part of a marginalized identity.

I watched as the officer skimmed over the multipage letter, which now was a slightly offset copy. He took a pen out of his breast pocket, along with a notebook, and started to jot down some numbers and notes. He asked us several questions, the answers we gave him all blurred together. We felt drugged, everything was moving in slow motion.

"Okay, I want you to call the number I have written down on this piece of paper and give them the case number I am assigning you." He handed us a small two-by-four-inch piece of paper that now had frayed edges from where it was torn from the spiral wire.

"Who do we talk to when we call?" I asked as I looked down at the scribbles.

"A detective that works on harassment cases," he replied.

I looked at him; hearing those words out loud from a police officer gave me hope that something could be done. I watched as he got up from the stool and put his notepad back into his breast pocket. With each movement, his leather belt weighted down with a gun, handcuffs, bullets, and other accessories sounded like a leather saddle creaking with the motion of a horse. Before leaving, he scooped up the offset copy of the letter to place in his file. After the door closed behind him, Lily and I simultaneously let out long exhales. I turned from the door and looked at her. She had her arms crossed and was starting to chew on her right-index fingernail.

"Definitely going to be adding wine to the grocery list today," I said jokingly, but not jokingly. Being stalked was an additional notch of trauma in our lives that further increased both our anxiety and paranoia. Lily was starting to take a prescribed medication to help. I, however, chose medication that required fermentation before being packaged in bottles or cans.

△

After starting to date Lily, the online harassment that I experienced quickly increased, which was unusual. I hadn't been doing anything different: The only things that had changed were my zip code and being in a relationship with Lily. I tried to brush off the uptick of hateful comments or odd messages online as just different people being jealous, but then Lily received the voice mail followed by handwritten and typed letters arriving in our home's mailbox. The letter that arrived at Lily's office mirrored other letters we had received. In each, there were subtle comments about recent events Lily and I had gone to that were not advertised and things we had been involved with in our past. We both had targets on our back.

We knew we were being stalked. It was like the woman who had tipped Lily off a year ago; the culprits wanted us to know. We felt like mice that had been put in a cage with kittens. The cats were playing with us— gently enough *not* to kill us, but rough enough to make us feel completely debilitated.

A part of me wanted to look up to the sky, shake my fist, and yell, "Really, Universe? You haven't put me or Lily through enough in our lives?" I thought back to my eating disorder, coming out as lesbian and then transgender. I also thought about Lily's struggles to get through each day when an obsessed stalker wanted to ruin our careers, our relationship, and our lives. I hated that she was going through this, especially after hearing how the stalker was bringing up trauma Lily had experienced in her past. Incidents from her childhood and from a previous job, where the insurance rep sexually harassed her multiple times before he was fired, were thrown at her. It made my stomach double on top of itself when I thought about the very real risk and vulnerabilities that women face in this world due to men. I yearned for something to shift seismically after yelling this and to have all of the trauma and anxiety end, but I knew it wouldn't stop. I quickly started to become pissed off.

Lily and I were in the formative years of falling in love and trying to plan a life together, while fearing for our lives every day. No place felt safe, not Lily's office, our outings, or even being inside our home. Every car that drove by too slowly and every new vehicle parked on the street that didn't belong to our neighbors haunted us day and night. To make matters worse, being a national speaker meant I had a schedule posted on my website with when I would be out of town. Fearing ramped-up activity or someone harming Lily while I was gone, I took my schedules down and asked to have officers patrol our neighborhood and put surveillance on our home. The anxiety and fear we lived with could have pulled us apart, but it only strengthened our bond.

⚠

I started to notice that the stalker liked to reference a lot of things that could be found via an Internet search engine, so I decided to run a Google search of my name. I noticed that in the search results there was one that linked to a comment on my niece's YouTube channel. The comment was from "Ryan Sallans," but I did not put it there, nor did I have a YouTube channel under my legal name. A lump formed in my throat as I clicked on the link to read the imposter's comment. It was an anti-trans statement on my niece's page, which was concerning. For me, though, what was even more troubling was that this person had been following my online activity. No one would have known about my niece's YouTube channel, unless they saw something that I had posted about it.

I quickly ran a search on YouTube, only to discover this person had gone to other transgender individuals' YouTube channels, which I had visited, and had written more anti-trans statements. Not only did this person leave transphobic comments, but the imposter then got into arguments with other people in the comment section. With each posting, I felt my body go into full panic mode. I immediately took screenshots before reporting each comment as hate speech. I also reported the page, hoping that YouTube would quickly take it down. Discovering this reminded me why it was important to run an online search of my name from time to time. The ability for a stranger to impersonate another person is far too easy.

"911," a woman's monotone voice said.

"Please put me through to the nonemergency line," I stated before she could ask. It was sad that I was becoming an old hat at filing police reports.

When they file a report, police come to the location of the incident. In this case, they had to come to my home. As I watched the police cruiser pull up and then the officer walk up my front steps, I felt embarrassed. This was the second time they had visited our home to file a report. *What if the neighbors think I am abusing Lily?* The officer did the same thing each officer I worked with did; he collected information and wrote a case number on a two-by-four-inch piece of paper. It was another file that would go into another detective's desk drawer. When he left, I contacted a lawyer to help assure that YouTube removed the channel. Even when the page no longer existed, the concern for "what's next" hung in the background.

◬

The "what's next" was a small envelope arriving in our home's mailbox. A child's sloppy handwriting wrote out my address, no return address to be found. I looked at the red postmark placed on the outside of the envelope. The letter was mailed from a post office in the same city where we lived. Hoping I could catch the stalker, I ran to the kitchen and grabbed two ziplock bags. I didn't want to touch the letter inside, thinking the cops could swipe it for fingerprints, but what we see on TV is not how the real world works when it comes to detective work. I pulled out the letter and held it between the two Baggies. While the envelope's address appeared childlike, the letter inside was two paragraphs long, typed and printed. My hands shook as I read the words attacking my body and my work as an out trans man. The letter joined the previous ones we had received, locked away, inside their plastic Baggies, which have been dated, along with the sheets of paper with scribbled case numbers. I will not open them again. I will not rewrite what was written. I will not give them power over my life or Lily's life.

Stalkers want power. They want to see you squirm. They want to see you upset. They want you to interact with them so that they can remain in your life. Our stalker harassed us from when we first got together to the day we flew home from our one-year wedding anniversary. In the three years of experiencing this nightmare, Lily and I learned a lot about stalking and how to care for yourself when you are the victim. We learned that the officers, detectives, and victim advocates can be respectful, but not necessarily helpful. We learned that dealing with harassment and stalking requires a lot of documentation that provides sequential, hard, and tangible evidence. All the evidence we had collected was not seen as "hard enough." We learned that as victims, you begin to feel like people see you as being paranoid or as a conspiracy theorist.

To take what power we could over the situation, we learned that the best thing a victim can do is not engage. I also started an online policy of no engagement with people I viewed as bullies and harassers. Repeat offenders get blocked and then deleted. No matter how much you want to show your feelings or share things, do not engage and do not disclose. Continue with meticulous documentation, continue filing police reports, and hope that the stalker either loses interest or slips up over time and can finally be caught.

During the time of the stalking, we were determined not to let that person tarnish or overshadow our upcoming wedding. They wanted power, but we both refused to give it to them then, or any time that is left in our lives. The attempts at terrorizing us made me learn more about Lily's incredible strength. We always joked that if our relationship could last through the stalking, we knew we could make it through anything. It made me love Lily even more than I thought imaginable.

CHAPTER 8

GROOMED FOR THIS MOMENT

Selfie 87 – August 2012

I was sitting at another bar, in another airport. My trancelike stare studied the streaks of exposed wood grain—wood that used to be protected by layers of varnish now lying there, defenseless. It made me wonder how many years it had taken to wear down the protective surface, how many glasses had been pushed back and forth from different hurried or bored travelers. Even though it wasn't my counter, I instinctively wiped away the water ring left by my pint glass that sought a coaster. My brother, Greg, who clearly was not concerned by the water ring forming under his glass, was sitting on the stool to my left. Two hours ago, we had been sitting in front of cameras on a television show. Now we were next to an airline gate waiting to fly from New York back home to Nebraska. In five days, I would be marrying Lily in Colorado, but for this moment, I was sharing surreal aspects of my life with my brother. While we waited for our flight, I began to think back over the past two days.

△

The smell of gasoline fumes was a little overpowering as we stepped outside the arrival doors of LaGuardia Airport in New York City. I searched for the taxi that would be transporting us to Stamford, Connecticut, where the program would be filmed. After successfully identifying our ride and climbing into the backseat, I watched, with horror, as the cabby swerved through the traffic and tested out the accelerator and brakes at the same time. It was an experience I had only had before as a child in bumper cars. Fortunately, the cabby's goal was not to touch the other vehicles that were within millimeters of his car's yellow paint.

Although I lived in Nebraska, I was not a sheltered guy. I'd traveled all around the nation and had been to most of the big cities, but New York truly took the cake. The number of people, buildings, and times a person felt they must hit their car horn, while the thirty cars in front of them were also not moving, made me want to scream. I believed that if I ever lived in New York, I'd become the grouchy, hunched-over person who carried a phone with a honking car app on it, just to get people to move out of my way on the sidewalks. A hat tip to you, New Yorkers, for surviving mass chaos!

On this particular trip, my brother and I didn't get to experience the wonders that abound while navigating the city. Instead, we experienced a town that was a bit like a movie set, except it felt like nobody liked anyone else or felt the need to be anything but rude. That town is Stamford, Connecticut. Every restaurant Greg and I went to, every interaction with the hotel staff, felt like the space we occupied and air we breathed was off-putting. I am sure the people of Stamford are really wonderful—perhaps we were just there on an off-day.

The show that we were going to appear on was a different format from other talk shows that had interviewed me. The first realization that this experience would be different from some of my other television appearances was when we arrived at the studio. We were given a contract that included language about not bailing us out if we were put in jail prior to our appearance on the show. The second indicator was that on the morning of the show, we had to have a full pat down; then we had a metal detector run over our bodies and inspection of any bags that we brought into the studio. The third was having the legal department come in and videotape us answering some questions to clear the show of any liability. And the fourth? Hearing the screaming from people in a green room, adjacent to our own, who were going to be part of the second show they were filming that day.

It all came together for me when the producers were filming what is called "B-roll," film that doesn't have a narrative but connects a story. For my B-roll, they wanted to film me lifting weights in a tank top and then flexing my biceps. This felt odd for me because I didn't consider myself a "fitness model" type, but I agreed to it. They took me up to a room where there was a rack of free weights, along with a treadmill and a gold-plated telescope used to look at stars and planets. It was an odd combination that had me scratching my head until the staff said, "You are in Jerry Springer's private room. You are the lucky one that gets to work out with his weights." I shook my head, still looking at the telescope, which didn't belong.

"That was a gift," one of the guys said while nodding his head in the direction of my gaze.

I was distracted by the telescope, so it took a few seconds for everything to sink in. *I am in Jerry Springer's private workout room. We are in the same studio that produces Jerry's show.* This most likely meant the same producers were working on the show that I would soon be interviewed on. I had no clue where my brother was during the filming of the workout session. When I was taken to our green room, my brother was not present, but I was joined by comedian Ian Harvie and musician Rocco Kayiatos. We hung out in the green room for two hours before being lined up to be brought onto the stage. We could hear a person speaking loudly over the microphone, getting the live audience excited and riled up. I began to wonder, *Are we getting ready to go on a talk show or out into the Coliseum to fight gladiators?* While standing there, the host, Trisha Goddard, greeted us.

As she shook my hand, she jokingly said in her British accent, "Oh, Ryan, you look a lot like my ex-husband. We may have a bit of a problem."

I knew she was kidding around with me. If I were better at having good comebacks, I could have said, "You have good taste." But I didn't know how to react, so I just awkwardly giggled.

After walking onstage, we were instructed to sit on stools, which faced a large audience—an audience that had been bused in from New York City for the show. They initially wanted the opening to be a shock-and-awe moment, where they would have two other guys who were not trans men sit with us, and then tell the audience (who didn't know the topic) that three of the men onstage were born women. When they pitched this idea to Ian, Rocco, and me, we adamantly stated we would not participate in the show if they proceeded forward. Fortunately, they listened and went a different direction. The episode turned out to be one of the best interviews I had been a part of, with the most memorable part being when they asked my brother to stand up in the audience and answer a couple of questions from the host.

"That transition, was that a shock to you?" Trisha asked while standing next to Greg.

He was wearing a bright purple shirt, which was on loan to him from the show. The person dressing us didn't like the options he had brought. I had to look past the obscenely purple color to focus on what he was saying.

"It was probably like a deer caught in the headlights. I was like, what the hell, and then I got in my car and drove home, and I just started freaking bawling . . ." He paused, his voice started to crack. "'Cuz, you know, it was like what the hell is going on here. This is my sister."

The host shook her head, connecting with the emotions my brother was starting to show as his voice cracked. "Are you proud of your brother?"

"Oh, God, yeah, he does so much in educating the community, businesses, and schools, and that is so important because I see all this mindless hate and bigotry . . . it's ignorance." The audience broke out in a unison clap. After our segment, Greg and I were rushed out of the studio so that we could catch our flight back to Nebraska.

The high we were both on from the show led us to the airport bar. We still had an hour before our flight would board. If anyone looked at us sitting next to each other, one could easily tell we were brothers. Of course, it didn't help that we were both wearing gray button-up shirts (he had changed back to his clothes before we left the studio), and we had our hair cut and styled exactly the same way by the hairstylist who worked for the TV show. I thought back to the moment I sat in the hairstylist's chair prior to going on-air. As he pulled out his clippers, I realized whatever cut he gave me would forever be immortalized in my wedding photos, which was just five days away.

He placed the two-gauge on the razor and began running it up the sides of my head, giving me a semi-high and tight haircut like the military, which I was somewhat okay with. I became quickly not okay when he took the same razor and pressed it against my neckline. As the swoops went up, so did the strands of hair that were part of my beautiful beard. I quickly transformed into the lion in the cartoon *The Lion, the Witch and the Wardrobe* that lost its beautiful mane . . . only I wasn't tied down by little creatures and tortured. My stomach flipped over each time he ran the razor along my face. I prided myself in having a full beard that covered my cheeks, jawline, and part of my neck. I also have a small chin, so the beard added length to my face. The stylist trimmed it in a way that made me look a bit like one of the characters from the MTV reality show *Jersey Shore.*

"Keep it short and clean, it looks better," he said to me.

I just shook my head in disbelief. I didn't want to look clean. I wanted to look like a mountain man. After all, I was getting married in the mountains.

△

I caught my brother's and my reflection in the mirror behind the bar. I realized if my dad had been sitting next to us, our features would all blend together.

"Hey, when you have a second, could you take a picture of us?" I asked the bartender, who was plunging glasses into the sink to rinse them of their previous beverages. I often wonder how clean the pint glasses are that we all drink out of when we are at a bar. Does plunging them in soapy water for a second, and then cold water for another, really clean them?

"Sure," he said as he set the glasses down on a rubber mat to dry. He came around from the bar to get a better angle and took a few photos for us to pick from. I looked at my brother and just smiled. It wasn't too often that I got to spend time with him. It also was special for me to be able to share a piece of my life with him, which included a lot of travel and the occasional TV appearance. With most people, you get a pretty good feel for what their life and occupation feel like because you've seen it or experienced it yourself. What I do is a little more rare.

"Just think, in a few days we'll be together again, only this time we'll be in Colorado!" Along with having my brother experience a piece of my work life, I was also excited for him, and everyone else attending, to see Lily's and my special place in the mountains.

"Oh, right, yeah. I can't believe that is this weekend already." He took a sip of his beer. "Do you think Dad's head is going to explode?"

His question made my giddiness pause.

△

Just two weeks prior, I wasn't even sure if my parents would be coming to my wedding. My dad had found three copies of my first book, *Second Son,* on my brother's bookshelf. He had never read it, but he pulled a copy off the shelf and read a section about our family's hardships. He did not like the few paragraphs he had read. I learned this after finding an e-mail from him that popped up in my in-box. In the e-mail, he pointed out the sections that he read were not accurate, according to his memories. For me and my memories, they were.

Except one. In my first edition of *Second Son*, I had written that my parents were going to name me Jareth, if I were born assigned male. My dad pointed out that they were going to name me Jarod Lee. After he pointed this out, I thought back to how I came up with Jareth for the name and realized that my dad was right. In fact, I remember in second grade when I asked them what they would have named me, they said Jarod. The next day at school, I was on the swing set during recess, thinking about the name Jarod, and decided that wasn't cool enough. I wanted to be named Jareth. This was a name that I had gotten from the movie *Labyrinth.* When the second edition of *Second Son* was released, I corrected that error. Beyond getting my name wrong, my dad was so upset that he expressed that it may be best for him not to come to our wedding.

His e-mail left me feeling shrunken and disposed of. While our relationship wasn't perfect, while we still had a lot of work to do to gain comfort around one another, I was no longer written out of the family. I had hoped that having my parents at my wedding would push us into a new space of acceptance and form a happy memory of us all together, post-transition. To not have them there would make me feel like we were going back to square two in our relationship. Square one was complete disownment, which we passed after a year into my transition. Square two was acknowledging we were alive and family, but not interacting with each other except for two hours, once a year. After announcing my engagement to Lily, we had started to move to square three, which was still infrequent communication, but we saw each other twice a year, for two to four hours per visit.

Lily tried to soothe me by saying, "Weddings always bring out the chaos in families."

I knew my dad's reaction could be just that, or perhaps he was also feeling hurt because Lily and I didn't include them in the planning of our wedding. The thought hadn't crossed my mind, since they weren't a huge part of my life after receiving my undergraduate degree. So, eleven years later, I didn't know how to incorporate them into major events.

A part of me wanted to write back to my father, *Fuck you, don't come.* But I knew that wasn't the truth; I couldn't imagine my wedding without my parents in attendance. Instead of letting anger or hurt feelings lead my reaction, I tried to step into his shoes for a minute to understand what may be going on inside his mind and heart.

While I am only a parent of four-legged fur children, I can still recognize that parenting human children is not easy and is extremely complicated. Managing your own feelings and stress, while also guiding children for whom you are responsible, is hard. Having children who have different views than yours also presents a challenge, but one that hopefully would allow for conversation, growth, and appreciation.

Thinking back to my relationship with my parents, I transitioned prior to the coverage or support that exists today around transgender identities. I transitioned in a family rooted in the Midwest, with older parents who didn't understand the topic or how it works. I transitioned and publicly shared my story. This was a huge challenge for my father, who was a proud man. Over the years, he improved with processing his feelings, but I believe my book brought up everything he had felt when I first began my journey. I assumed he experienced hurt, anger, confusion, fear, loss, and feeling unappreciated as a father.

I e-mailed him, sharing my feelings. He responded to me:

Some people have a goodness inside of them that glows and attracts others to them. You have always been one of those rare individuals. You were a good kid, fun to be with, a hard worker, and an excellent student. Now you have found someone to share your life, and your mom and I couldn't be happier for you. We have thought the world of Lily ever since we met her, she has that glow also. In your e-mail, you said that you felt that I was angry with you about your book. I wasn't angry, just very sad. I was sad that your perception and recollection of your childhood was so horrible and that you were so unhappy. I know that I wasn't a great father,

81

but I really did try. I guess it shows how one person's memory of an event is so different from another. My only memories of you as a child was that of a great kid that I truly enjoyed being around and thought we had a good, close relationship. I evidently was wrong.

My dad's e-mail made me think about a trip to Amsterdam that I had taken with Lily. During our trip, we had the great privilege of going to Anne Frank's house and walking through the small, dark rooms on the top floor of a warehouse. These rooms were her family's place of hiding for two years before the Nazis found them, tore the family apart, and forced them into concentration camps. Anne's frail body and spirit reached a point where she lost her battle for survival, a point that was just two weeks shy of the camps being stormed and the people—starving and sick—saved by the liberating armies. Her father, Otto, was the only person in her family of four who survived. After walking through the rooms, bare of furniture to respect the family's experience and life within those walls, you find yourself back on the first floor. On this floor, there is a large display including interviews with Otto. As an old man, he reflected upon his feelings when he read his daughter's diary.

"You'll never really know your children," he said while thinking about the words she had inscribed into diaries that would later be shared around the world. Hearing Otto say that made me pause and think about my own family. I feel it is natural for parents to assume they are going to be able to relate and understand their kids. When thinking about couples that have a biological child, from the instant the child is born, families are looking for similarities. In my household, I heard things like:

"Oh, you have your father's eyes."

"You laugh just like your mother."

"You hold your fork like ..."

We look for what joins us, what things we see that feel familiar, so that we can understand something outside ourselves. I would have assumed, living in the same tiny space for two years, never being able to leave, the Franks would have been closer. However, even in their situation, there was mystery, feelings left unspoken or unshared.

People ask me how I forgave my family for how I was treated when I came out as transgender. This is a question that makes me stop and pause. I do not have the desire to forgive my family for actions from their past. Those actions have created wounds that, for me, simply can't be healed by saying, "I forgive you." I recognize that no person is perfect. No family exists where everyone comes out unscathed, either emotionally or physically. All human beings, no matter how good they are, have done something that in present time would be labeled as offensive, wrong, or not the best one could do. This is part of being human. The hope is that we can learn from past mistakes and work to do better.

I can physically see that my family is changing with each year that passes, but internally we all still have notches in our bones and nicks in our hearts. I assume my parents still have feelings of fear around when I was emaciated, and feelings of loss due to their child changing from female to male, Kim to Ryan, her to him. Internally, my teenage spirit still carries feelings of abandonment; my young-adult spirit harbors feelings of being unwanted; my adult spirit has feelings of being a stranger in familiar land. The old voices once told me, *"No one will notice if you are gone. You do not matter in this world."* These voices still have a stage and have fueled my ongoing depression, eating disorder thinking, drinking, and loneliness.

To help comfort me and help me remember a loving and unscathed parent-child connection, I have set pictures on my bookcase: one of me as a four-year-old child wrapping my arms around my mom, both of us with smiles that run the full expanse of our faces. Another picture is perched on a shelf showing my tiny body clad in my cowboy hat and boots. I'm sitting on a horse next to my dad, who is also adorned in a cowboy hat and boots. I keep those photos in plain sight to remind me continually of the parent-child relationship that will forever be stored under our skin and within our hearts. I am also fortunate to have Lily beside me, but like Otto's realization, Lily is not always aware of some of my darkest thoughts and times where I feel so alone and unanchored. I had hoped marrying Lily would help make me feel anchored and connected to something outside myself. I had hoped that having my parents at the wedding would help us form new bonds and memories, while overpowering old wounds.

After two weeks of phone conversations with my mom and e-mails to my dad, they agreed to join us in Colorado.

△

On our wedding day, the weather started out with blue skies. This was important, since it was an outdoor ceremony in the backyard of Elizabeth's house. As we reached the afternoon, dark clouds started to roll in and over the mountain range. I kept looking out the front window, nervously watching the dark clouds, while also looking out toward the backyard, where the skies were still blue. One of our friends saw my furrowed eyebrows and anxious expression, so she grabbed me by both shoulders and calmly said, "Do not worry. Everything will be fine."

"Uh-huh," I unsurely responded. To me, those big-ass clouds hovering over a valley, with black streaks going from sky to ground, weren't signs of things going fine.

"You know, if it rains, it is a sign of good luck on a wedding day."

I wasn't sure if she was just blowing smoke up my ass, or if that was true, but the effort to calm me down was appreciated. "Thank you," I said. "I think I'm just going to go get ready."

"That sounds like a good idea," she replied. She patted both of my shoulders, in a way that felt like she also wasn't so sure of her words. Her action felt like she was the boss man in the Mafia trying to calm me down before I got filled with bullets shot through a closed door. Only, this time around, the bullets would be rain pellets on my head. I turned from her and the windows and walked toward the guest bathroom.

Everything is going to be okay, I repeated to myself as I pulled my gray slacks on. *Everything is going to be great!* I decided I needed to ramp up the positivity in the room. Looking at my reflection in the mirror, I was happy to see that my beard had grown out a bit since the talk show. My look had shifted from being on *Jersey Shore* to selling Jersey Shore real estate. On the door behind me, my white dress shirt, gray vest, and tie were hung. I looked at my naked torso before pulling the shirt off the hanger. As I pushed each button through its respective hole, it hit me: *I am marrying Lily. She is marrying me.*

While I finished dressing, I thought about her also getting ready across the street at the neighbor's house. It was our final moments apart, our final moments of being single. Our wedding was not traditional, but we had decided (because of my own superstitions) that I would not see her until we were ready to walk down the aisle, or, in this case, up the stone steps to the pergola. We would marry in the same spot where, two years prior, I had made my proclamation; the same spot where, one year prior, I had proposed.

After my third attempt in tying a nice knot in my tie, I took one more look at myself in the mirror. When I was an adolescent, it was hard for me to imagine myself as a bride marrying someone. As I moved into my late-teenage years, I always imagined myself getting married outside in the mountains or cliffside. It felt surreal to think back to my daydreams of my wedding day as a young woman, compared to the reality of a thirty-three-year-old man. What I hadn't imagined is that instead of wearing basketball shorts and shoes under a dress (which I planned to take off immediately after saying "I do"), I would have a beard and be in a suit with sneakers. The different paths and journeys that we all take in life are fascinating.

It was time for guests to start arriving for our cocktail party. Over the past year, Lily and I had earmarked our favorite love songs and then burned those onto a CD, which would play over the speakers as people drank cocktails and ate cheese. My brother and his girlfriend were the first to arrive. Like me, he always showed up a half hour to fifteen minutes early to any event. I've learned over the years that if something starts at one o'clock, I will tell him to come at one-thirty.

As they walked up to the front door, I noticed that my brother was wearing blue jeans, flip-flops, and a black T-shirt with Bill Murray's face on it. I just shook my head. Greg is Greg, and I love him for that, but it also made me angry at how society treats boys versus girls. Growing up, I tried to wear clothes that I was comfortable in, only to be told by my parents to go change because I looked like a slob, and that it wasn't ladylike. Greg shows up at my wedding in a T-shirt, blue jeans, and flip-flops, and no one even blinks an eye.

As more guests arrived, I kept looking out the window for my parents' car to roll up. After everything we had been through the past few weeks, I just wanted to see their faces, hoping they would show approval of me. When I saw their gray Buick pull up into the driveway, I swung the front door open to greet them and my sister.

"Welcome!" I said.

"Thanks," my dad replied as he closed the door to his car. I walked up to him and gave him a brief, one-pat hug.

"We made it!" my mom said before letting out a small laugh. She walked around the car to give me a hug; this hug lasted a little longer.

"Happy wedding day! . . . I'm sick," my sister, Debra, said with a smile, then a frown, as she gave me a small hug.

My family is just like me, socially awkward when first arriving at social events, especially if the event involved people they did not know. I've learned not to take offense by the semi-awkward hugs and greetings, because after getting acclimated, the interactions would change. I escorted them with the other guests to the patio; food and booze always lighten the anxious tension.

A photographer—well, the neighbor boy from next door who was learning how to do photography—ran around like he was behind the scenes, snapping candid photos for our memories. Several of the photos captured me on my tiptoes, bear-hugging my father, who stood three inches taller. The smile on my face resembled those from my childhood when my dad would take me out horseback riding, or when he would have me sit on his lap and grab the wheel of our old Chevy pickup as it went down the roads, rolling hills with loose gravel on top, near our home.

My mom and sister sat at one of the round tables as the hour passed by. Debra had a tissue tucked into her hand, battling a respiratory infection. She looked like she could really use a warm bed and a glass of pinot, or in this case maybe a shot of the hard stuff to try and kill whatever viral infection sat inside her body. I walked over to them; they were engaged in a conversation with one another. My mom looked up, her gaze went from my head to my feet and back to my head. While in midsentence, she stopped, then said, "You look very nice, by the way."

Growing up, I had rarely heard my parents say those words to me when it came to my appearance and formal events. Hearing it now, I felt validated. I wanted to exclaim, "See! THIS is how I wanted to dress as a kid, but you wouldn't let me! Imagine how many less fights we would have had if you just let me present in a way that I felt comfortable." But I kept this as an inside thought, and instead just said, "Thank you."

I had been given the stamp of approval. It made me wonder how my past would have been, and how I would feel in my body currently, if I had been able to dress in the clothes that felt right for me as a child. How different would things have been if I had not received lectures about how it was inappropriate or how it looked sloppy? I knew I had to find a way to let those past experiences go, to stay focused on the present, but wiping away the grit can take more than just one pass.

I looked up to the sky. It was still blue above us, and to the south, the dark clouds had pushed west. The wind that had been blowing had settled, and it was time for the formal ceremony to begin. I ran inside to change the music for our wedding march. Instead of a piano playing "Here Comes the Bride," we chose a song by Alexi Murdoch titled "Wait." The acoustic guitar began to play while our thirty guests surrounded the pergola and got settled. They all turned their attention to me, standing alone by the glass doors. Alexi's voice was quiet at first, his lyrics sang about finding his identity and strength while fumbling through the messiness of humanity.

As his voice rose with the pace of the song, and he asked the woman he loved to wait for him as he gained more strength in self, the glass doors swung open. Lily gracefully stepped out and in front of me. I stood, stunned. Her long legs were covered by a shining gold material with draped singlet pieces of cloth that flowed separately from one another. Her eyelashes perfectly curled upward and downward, accentuating her mysterious dark brown eyes. Her small shoulders and clavicle bones held up the bodice of her dress with an exposed back. She truly looked like a Greek goddess.

Tears entered both of our eyes as we forgot about the wedding and everyone around us. We grabbed each other's hands and smiled. She nodded to me by blinking; I could tell she was nonverbally saying, *Are you ready?* I nodded my head, and we both took a couple breaths before dropping one set of hands. We turned and faced our guests; hummingbirds swirled around us, seeking flower nectar. Together, we walked up the path to start a new chapter in our lives.

I'll always hold Lily's and my wedding as a sacred day. It was a day that our close friends and family continue to say was one of the best weddings they had ever attended. We chose to have a small wedding, a wedding where we asked people not to post pictures on social media. I want to honor the requests we had then by not providing all the details with readers now. Our wishes reflected what Lily and I have always held true with one another: Beyond our work, small, intimate moments with friends and family are what matter most in our lives.

I will share that after we kissed and began our walk back down the steps from the pergola, I let Lily take the lead, and I held her hand to help steady her. As we lifted up our arms to see what step we took next, the neighbor-boy photographer snapped something unexpected. In the photo, he had perfectly captured the sun, as if it was resting between our held hands, bracing us as we guided each other down the path.

Photo by Hunter Lea

CHAPTER 9

MORTALITY IS CALLING

Selfie 98 – July 2013

"Fuck, fuck, fuck!" Lily screamed as tears streamed down her face. She shifted her weight from side to side, constricted by the seat belt holding her in place. I didn't want to leave. My mind was racing with different excuses as to why we should stay, but I knew all would be trumped.

We had to go back.

That morning we received a call from her mom where we learned that Lily's grandfather, a man that was like a father to her, was dying. The fine lines on Lily's face were beginning to turn coarse, and the furrow of my brow was close to permanently stuck. My knuckles turned white as I gripped the steering wheel and firmly pressed my foot against the accelerator of my Jeep.

"I just want to be home!" she yelled.

I remained quiet and had to remind myself to breathe as I swerved in and out of traffic. It was supposed to be a getaway, an unplugged weekend spent relaxing in the wilderness. It was our first time camping together, a fact that I didn't like to think of, since I used to be an avid outdoor adventurist. With my transition, all of my external adventures stopped as I unwound my internal paths. My adventures turned from the outdoors to the next physical step in my transition: a surgery, another shot of hormones, a legal document that needed to be changed. My life had become consumed by me being reborn into myself. Having transitioned several years ago, I was trying to do a new transition of finding my playful spirit again. This was an adventure I didn't have to travel alone, since Lily was also ready to find life outside of work and grappling identities.

Many people joke about Nebraska and how it must be flat and plain, but it is one of the most geographically diverse states in the nation. In the middle of the state, you have the rolling plains, but those are buffered by the Loess Hills to the east, deposited after the Ice Age by windblown dust, and the Sandhills to the west, home now to ranchers and cattle. Our trip led us to a spot west of the Missouri River, cornered by Iowa and South Dakota.

The state park was nestled by trees, hills, and skies speckled with white cumulous clouds. We drove through the archway of trees and up steep hills. Campsites were filling up with families in tents and campers. We kept driving up the winding hills until we reached a site with only two distant tents in sight. Within a few minutes of setting up camp, we saw two small deer prancing through the adjacent cornfield, only to shoot around and out of sight upon noticing us gawking at them. I reached out my hand and grabbed Lily's. She looked over at me, her dark eyes held my gaze as I looked at her, hoping she would see another aspect of who I was and what I wanted us to be. We weren't even a year into our marriage, but were already suffering from the mundane familiarity of each other's company.

△

When we first started dating, I quit my job as a health educator to become a professional speaker. To celebrate, Lily wanted to surprise me by making reservations at an elegant restaurant, the kind where you have to wear a jacket or tie, otherwise you won't be allowed in. The server, dressed in a black tie and a wrinkle-free white dress shirt, escorted us to a small round table set in the middle of the room. The only light provided was candlelight on the table and light shimmering from sconces on the walls. It was stuffy in there.

We both quickly felt out of place and were ready for the wine to be poured. Couples around us barely looked at each other or exchanged conversation. Instead, they had their smartphones placed firmly in front of their faces and thumbs moving up and down. Faces, lit by the glow, remained expressionless.

Lily and I looked at each other and, in unison, said, "I don't ever want us to be like that."

We both smiled while letting out a long, perfect, harmonious love sigh. Our smiles remained in place as we tilted our heads to the side and extended our arms across the table to hold each other's hands.

Well, we've become like that.

Okay, we've *sometimes* become like that. Not at restaurants, but at home. The mystery love bubble officially broke. Gone were the nice PJ's or the fantasy of lingerie; in were the pajama bottoms fraying out across the buttocks, material now held together by a thin line of stitching down the back. Instead of sitting and listening to music while engaging in stimulating conversation, I yearned for us to be in our den, where we could turn on the TV. It was a way to be together, but also to be checked out from reality. We had hit the point where we were more than comfortable with one another.

Our different endeavors when we were distracted from one another didn't mean we weren't in love with each other. It had just become easier to sit next to one another while scrolling through our phones, computers, or being distracted by the television. I started to recognize that I used the online world as my buffer so that I wouldn't have to talk about things that scared me about life. Lily used it because her schedule was always so busy that she simply needed to check out for a bit in order to recharge.

At first, I feared that we were going to end up exactly like the couples we saw at restaurants. However, after many arguments, and then conversations later about our arguments, we recognized how our online behaviors distracted us from life and each other. We've learned that when our distractions become too prominent, it is a sign that we need a vacation to unplug.

When on vacation, it was easier for me to unplug than it was for Lily. With her job as a therapist and with aging grandparents, she wanted to be available in case there was an emergency. I understood her reasoning, but it frustrated me when I saw her connection change within a millisecond of the phone ringing or dinging with a new text message.

⚠

Standing under the canopy of trees, we were lulled by the sounds of wind rattling the leaves and birds' chirped songs. I was getting ready to say, "I love you." I envisioned after I said those three words, we would embrace and melt into one another, making us feel as we had when we first fell in love. I was stopped by the *ding* of her phone, though. We were waiting for another couple to join us for the weekend and they needed some final directions. I gave up on the thought of us reconnecting and turned my attention to gathering small twigs for our evening fire.

That night, the campfire was hot, and the beer was cold. When it was time to retire for the evening, I got up and tipsily walked toward our tent. I quickly fell into a drunk sleep, the type of sleep where you crash hard, but then wake up and feel like you hadn't slept at all. The next morning, I went over to the stove and started to make coffee for my other camping companions. When the water started to bubble a dark brown into the glass top of the percolator, and the smell of freshly brewed coffee wafted into the tents, I heard rumblings of voices and the sound of zippers from sleeping bags.

"Dude, you snored so loud last night, I think you scared off any wildlife." I turned to see a head pop out of one of the tents.

"I did?" I asked, embarrassed and insecure.

"Yeah," he said, laughing. I knew Lily would not be laughing when she got out of the tent.

As we moved into our day, and farther into nature, I could feel Lily relaxing and letting go. We hiked along the river and took our shoes off to play on the sandbanks before traversing from water to land and up into the tree-covered hills, where we got lost from the poorly marked trails. The sweat, sun, sounds, and scents of nature made us all feel grounded, and made me feel connected to Lily again. After a horseback ride, we retired to our campsite for the evening, where we began playing with Wiffle balls and rackets while drinking beer. Lily's spirit felt light, open, and finally present, which gave me hope that tomorrow would be another great day. As we began to take another swat at the light and airy Wiffle balls, Lily's phone rang again. I hoped she wouldn't answer it, but the name on the caller ID was her mom's.

While talking, I noticed her light and playful spirit turn into a heavy, weeping wreck. Her mom was sharing the news that her grandpa was found unconscious in his apartment. The doctors were reporting that he had had a stroke and would most likely not come out of his unconscious state. The rackets we all held were dropped, along with the weekend escape. Lily's biggest fear about leaving for the weekend became a reality.

As we drove back to Omaha the next morning, I felt a mix of emotions. The leading emotion was guilt, shame, and greed for wanting Lily all to myself. The next was sadness for her soon-to-be loss, as well as all the emotions she was experiencing inside herself.

⚠

In July 2014, a year after her grandpa passed from a stroke, I received a similar call from my mom informing me that my grandma had been found at home on the ground, an apparent stroke was the culprit. Standing around her hospital bed, looking down at her, I felt déjà vu from our experience with Lily's grandpa. The one difference was that my grandmother was awake, unlike Lily's grandpa who had slipped into a coma. She could also still speak, even though half of her body was paralyzed. There was a feeding tube running out of her right nostril; medical tape on her face and chest kept the tube from bouncing around.

While my grandma could talk and still move her right side, she could not swallow. The doctors wanted to give her a couple more days to recover before having her do a swallow test. If she didn't pass, she wouldn't be leaving the hospital, and wouldn't be on this planet much longer. When I looked at her, I saw a reflection of what my future could bring. As we lose those that have always been there for us throughout our lives, we start to realize that we also will be in this place. I stared into my grandma's blue eyes and could tell that she knew she wouldn't be leaving the hospital in her physical body.

"I bet my hair looks terrible," she said as she lifted her good arm to touch the white down of hair that had recently been permed.

"Let me help you, Grandma," Debra said before walking over to her purse and pulling out a comb. Working as a cosmetologist in a salon that she owned, she was always prepared. As she brushed my grandma's hair, I found myself holding back the tears. Partly, because I didn't want people to see me cry, but also because I didn't want to alarm my grandma. I didn't want her to know that I was really scared.

My brother, who didn't like emotional moments, stood in the corner of the hospital room or paced back and forth. He found moments to crack jokes: "I guess this will impact your golf game." He did this partly as a defense to his own discomfort, but also to get my grandma to smile.

Lily was amazing. She sat by my grandma's side, stroked her bruised arms, and talked calmly with her while keeping her gaze locked on my grandma's face. This was a moment I took an internal snapshot of, since an actual photo of my grandma in a hospital bed felt weird. It would remind me that Lily's ability to love and be compassionate, when everyone else in the room just wanted to run away, was one of the things that tied my soul closer to hers.

Before we left the hospital, I leaned down to give my grandma a hug. I knew it might be our last. As I stood up, I said, "I love you, Grandma."

She looked at me and raised a half smile, impeded by one side being paralyzed from the stroke. "I will get better," she adamantly said through slightly slurred speech. "This is the pits." Her blue eyes did not blink as she said this; rather, they stayed locked on my face.

To this day, her words "this is the pits" both haunt and amuse me. She had just summed up life. A part of us wants to keep going, but eventually we realize we need to get off this ride.

Seven days later, I received a call from my mom. She had spent the past week at the hospital with her siblings. My grandma had failed the swallow test. As a result, the doctors removed her feeding tube. She lay in her hospital bed, starving to death, while her kids surrounded her. I can only assume that watching your mother die, slowly, is as painful as losing her.

"How are you doing, Mom?" the first question I asked after answering her call.

"I'm okay," she said, but her voice sounded tired. I could hear her footsteps echoing as she paced on the linoleum floor outside my grandma's hospital room. My mom, my brother, and I all have the habit of pacing while we talk on the phone. "Grandma still hasn't passed. I told her she just loves us so much, she doesn't want to leave us." She let out a weighted laugh.

Hearing my mom talk made me sad, not just for her and my grandma, but also from the idea of me being in her position one day. "I know this is hard. I love you, Mom."

"Love you, too."

"Please keep me updated."

"I will," she said.

Five minutes later, my phone rang again. "Mom?"

"Well, Mom decided it was time to go," she weakly said.

"Oh, no. I'm so sorry."

"It was time . . . she won't be in pain any longer."

⚠

My relationship with my parents started to turn a corner toward acceptance in 2009, after my dad's mom passed away. It was the first time I had heard my dad say, "This is my son Ryan." It was the first time they had seen me in a suit. It was the first time people in our small town could look at all of us and take in the changes I had undergone. I was asked to be one of the pallbearers at her funeral, a task traditionally assigned to men. They asked me to take on that task again at my grandma Margaret's funeral.

I decided it was time for me to purchase a new black suit. The suit I had worn in 2009 did not fit well. When I had purchased it from the clearance rack at Target, I had no clue what the numbers and letters meant regarding sizing. It looked like I had taken it out of my dad's closet. The sleeves hung over my hands, and the bottom of the pant legs had frayed from being caught under the heels of my shoes as I walked.

No one had taught me the art of men's formal-dress apparel. No one had taught me how I should button only the top button of the dress coat when standing and unbutton it when sitting. No one taught me how to place cuff links in the buttonholes at the bottom of the sleeves. No one taught me how to properly tie a tie and what the different knots looked like.

I had been left to figure everything out on my own: from how to buy and wear clothes, to how to properly shave so that I didn't have ingrown hairs on my neck. I could ask someone for help, but a guy in his thirties asking for help around grooming and apparel felt emasculating to me. As ridiculous as it was, I had to keep my "man pride."

The morning of my grandma's funeral, I was looking in the mirror, tongue sticking out to the side of my mouth while I attempted to get my tie placed so that the front part dangled just below my belt line. Right then, I received a text from my brother: *Dude, do you have a tie I can borrow?* This text wasn't a surprise. It came from a guy who had worn a T-shirt decorated with Bill Murray's face to my wedding. I looked in my closet, ties for different seasons and occasions hung on wood pegs. I had first started purchasing these ties just nine years ago. Lucky for him, I had purchased two black ties for formal events. I texted him back: *Yep, I'll give it to you when I pick you up.*

When we arrived at the funeral, my brother got out of the car and looked at his reflection in the passenger window to assist with tying a Windsor's double knot. While we stood in the summer's sunlight, a large pickup pulled up next to us. As the door swung open, we noticed it was our brother-in-law, Kasey, and my sister, Debra. We gave each other hugs before my sister walked up to the church to find our parents. Her husband remained with us and began to make small talk. My brother completed his Windsor knot and turned to face us both. Kasey looked at my brother's knot and then looked at mine. "Dude, how did you tie that thing?"

I quickly became embarrassed, another sign that I was not raised male. Moments like this, I became paranoid, fearing that people were thinking, *Even though Ryan has transitioned, he is obviously not a man. He doesn't even know how to tie a tie!*

"What do you mean?" I asked while trying to push out my paranoid thinking.

"Come here, let me show you how to do it." His fingers started to pull apart my knot, followed by instructions on how to run the large part, placed to the right of my neck over and under the thinner part of the cloth draped on the left side of my neck. I had been doing it right, only in reverse. "There you go," he said as he took a step away from me.

"Thanks" is all I could get out, still afraid that they were questioning my male identity.

We walked into the funeral and sat down. As the ceremony started, I instantly became uncomfortable. The minister, a guy who couldn't be a year out of seminary school, started harping on how we were all sinners. When he said, "Margaret was a sinner," I about jumped out of the pew to scream at him. His words were not celebrating my grandma's life. She was not a sinner; she was a person we all loved.

My grandma was the person who taught me about the wilderness, and when I was a child, she bought me my first pair of binoculars. She was a person who donated her land to Nebraska's Audubon Society. That land was then turned into one of the most frequented locations in the nation for people to come from around the world to watch the Sandhill crane migration. As he continued with his fire-and-brimstone rant, I wanted to yell, "Shut up!" But I just sat there because the other one hundred people in the room also sat there.

"Let's sing a hymn," the minister said.

I looked down at the pew in front of me, expecting to see a bookshelf where the hymnals and Bibles usually were placed, but there were no books. Looking back up, I saw the words had been projected onto a screen above the minister's head. As the organ began to blow out the chords to guide us, my brother leaned over to me and said, "What is this, Jesus karaoke?" I couldn't hold in my laughter on this sad day. It was a release I needed at that moment, a release of joy and smiles that I hoped my grandma's spirit could feel.

As the sermon wrapped up, all of us men who were chosen as the pallbearers—my brother and a couple of our cousins—walked out to a van that would be driving us to the cemetery. An elderly man was our chauffeur. He grunted as he climbed into the van and positioned himself behind the wheel. When he turned the key in the ignition, a blasting voice on the radio followed the roar of the engine.

I quickly learned it was a talk-radio station playing. I hate talk radio. To Lily's chagrin, I hate podcasts. I hate anything where I have to sit and listen without being able to see the person speaking because it is hard for me to hear the words. Even when it comes to music lyrics, I know maybe 20 percent of any song, and of that, only 5 percent of the lyrics I sing are right.

As the van carried us away from the church and through the rural town, a loud man's voice came through the speakers. "If you can't speak English, you shouldn't be a customer service agent," he said. As his commentary grew more and more into a rant about immigration, I looked over to everyone else in the car and sighed. We had gone from a sermon talking about sinners to anti-immigration, Lord help us all.

"Excuse me," I said as I leaned over the driver's shoulder. "Can you turn the radio off, please?"

"Turn it up? Sure!" he replied before leaning over to turn the knob. *"You can't understand a damn thing they say . . ."* The asshole's voice vibrated my bones. My brother broke into laughter, while my blood pressure rose.

"No," I said loudly. "Off. Please turn it off."

"Oh," he said apologetically. "Sorry."

The radio went silent. I again looked at everyone in the car. My brother continued to laugh, but the other faces were stoic.

At the cemetery, all of our faces became stoic as we carried the casket to my grandma's final resting place. In my hand, I tightly gripped the metal bar that was attached to the coffin on a horizontal plane. The weight pulled on my shoulder, this casket was heavier than the one that contained my grandma Verna. I walked carefully, not wanting to stumble on the uneven ground. I needed to prove that I could handle the weight and the pressure, that I was just as much of a man as my cousins and brother. We set her down and I took several steps back, stopping at a place that joined me back with my family. My dad looked down to me and patted me on the shoulder pad of my black jacket. I looked up at him and then back over to where I had just placed my grandma.

The shine on the wood casket started to become muted as people placed flowers on top; a tombstone stood behind the large box. Her name had already been engraved into the stone. Next to her name was the worn lettering that spelled out my grandpa Louie's. I had no memory of him, since he had died of a heart attack when I was two years old. In looking at their names next to each other, I thought about their souls. If there was an afterlife, I hoped they could find happiness together after thirty-three years of being apart.

$$\triangle$$

Lily's grandmother's soul soon joined her grandfather's. Three grandparents, three important people in our lives, were lost so quickly and in a row. They had brought us happiness, and we can only hope that we did the same for them. The deaths of our grandparents wrenched our hearts. There are still days when both Lily and I will stop what we are doing, look at each other with tears in our eyes, and say, "I miss my grandparents."

We both wonder if at those times our grandparents are near us, watching us, or if we just have a memory that makes us wish they were near. Their deaths saddened me but did not put me in shock. Their deaths were different. I wasn't ready, both spiritually and mentally, for what would become one of the hardest deaths in my life.

We both evident in those that our grandparents are nearing interment. Yet it weighs me more than hitherto, they were near. The death saddens me but different: man speak, their lives differently, wrapped away, both spiritual, emotionally, on what would become one of the hardest death in my life.

CHAPTER 10

TEARING DOWN THE WALLS . . .
LITERALLY AND EMOTIONALLY

Selfie 103 – November 2013

Only a few leaves still clung to the thin branches of the birch trees that surrounded the bay. It was a postcard-perfect day—a day when fall was being encapsulated by winter's gray skies, a breeze that required one more layer over a sweater, but not gloves. It was a day where a warm fireplace and hot chocolate, with marshmallows melting on top, made you feel comforted. The foreign sound of seagulls beckoned my attention away from the trees, and toward the calm bay, where boats rocked slowly back and forth. Small ripples ran away from the curvature of the hull.

Having grown up in Nebraska, when I look out over the water, I always feel like a child. I stand in wonder of the unknown both below the water and stretching out over the horizon. In a few hours, I would be speaking at a university in Rhode Island. For now, I was just a tourist.

My childlike trance was broken by a small beep. I had forgotten to put my phone on silence. I opened up my messenger box to find a message from a former colleague at the University of Nebraska-Lincoln. It was only two sentences long, two sentences that would forever be etched into my memory: *I was wondering if you heard about Karen. Let me know.*

It was just after one in the afternoon, everything around me slowed to a pause and began to go into reverse. I turned away from the bay and started to stumble toward my hotel while thinking about the message I had just received. Karen had been the nutritionist I saw for several years while working on my recovery from my eating disorder. The first day I met her, I was a frail shell of my former self. Nineteen years old, thin to the point of being near hospitalization, I was scared.

Karen was a woman in her early forties, but from her appearance, she felt older to me. Her thin, burnt-amber hair was cut just above her shoulders, and parted down the middle, no bangs. She was wearing khaki slacks cut like mom jeans, and had a red sweater covering her small shoulders. I never knew if she liked to wear red because it was her favorite color or because it was one of our university's colors. Karen was a small woman, both in height and body size. Her weight sometimes made me wonder if she also had a past history with an eating disorder, but I didn't feel that was an appropriate question to ask.

Over the next six years, our relationship grew. She started as my nutritionist, instructing me to write food journals and bring them to our weekly meetings. I hated those journals. She then became a co-facilitator of a support group I was forced to participate in, guided by *The Don't Diet, Live-It! Workbook*. She then shifted into my advisor for two eating disorder education groups. And lastly, she was a colleague at UNL's health center, where I worked as a graduate assistant. After my graduations from undergraduate and graduate programs, she became a dear friend.

In looking back at seven out of my eight years of college, I couldn't remember a day where Karen wasn't in my life. My heart stopped and automatically I thought she had been in a terrible accident. My thumbs fumbled with my phone: *What about Karen? Now I am worried.*

The worst thing about texting is waiting. I stood there and stared at my screen, heart now racing, head spinning, breath heavy. "Come on, Jen!" I yelled at my phone, hoping it would prompt the three dots to start to bounce in the text box. Remembering the old saying "A watched pot never boils," I set my phone down and began pacing my hotel room. My feet started to follow the lines and patterns that kept forming into triangles in the carpet. Meanwhile, I kept my ear perked for the *ding* from my phone. Time slowed to what felt like ten years, even though it was just minutes.

I walked back over to my phone to find that Jen had just sent a reply. It was a cut-and-paste message that Karen had sent out a week prior to everyone at the health center. The two words "pancreatic cancer" stood out from the rest of the information Karen had shared. I felt a moment of relief, knowing that she had not been killed in an accident, but then I went into total shock. I hadn't lost her that day, but I knew I would lose her very soon. While I was able to recover from my eating disorder, sort of, you don't recover from pancreatic cancer.

I let my phone drop to the floor while I fell onto the bed. In two hours, a student would be picking me up from my hotel. In two hours, I would be presenting in front of a room full of people, sharing a story of recovery, transitioning, and finding self. With a lifetime of practice, I had perfected stuffing my feelings and putting on a show, which I did that night.

⚠

After being dropped back off at my hotel, I felt restless. I couldn't sit in my room, so I wandered over to a pub across the street and ordered a Guinness. Drinking an Irish beer made me think about Karen. We both bonded over our Irish heritage. I looked around at everyone in the pub, smiling, laughing, touching one another, feeling loved. I couldn't wait any longer. I pulled out my phone and dialed Karen's number. This was one of the few phone calls I've made in my life where I wanted the person to pick up the phone instead of me just leaving a voice mail.

"Hello?" Her voice sounded tired. This was not her first call for the day or week.

"Hey, Karen!" I tried to keep my voice more upbeat. "I am in Rhode Island and thought I would just call you to . . . check . . . in . . ." I failed, because my voice started to crack.

"You know, don't you?" She was matter-of-fact.

"Yes." I began to bawl.

"You never know. I could go into remission. I met a guy today while waiting for my chemo treatment who is now into his third year of treatment and he looks great." Her voice didn't sound as optimistic as her words.

"I really love you, Karen." Tears started to stream down my face.

"I love you, too."

I hung up the phone, knowing it would be one of our last conversations. My streak of tears instantly turned into an ugly cry—a body-convulsing, snot-running-down-over-my-mustache cry. My dad's voice, which was really society's voice, told me to stop: "Men don't cry."

"Shut up!!!" I yelled to myself. I was angry that I was feeling embarrassed by having strangers see me cry while sitting alone in an Irish pub, slurping a Guinness. I was angry that this type of messaging is used in our society to make a person a "man." We all should be able to express and embrace our emotions; that is the one thing that can join us all together.

⚠

As Karen was in her final week of life, my anger toward everything grew stronger. To try and let out the emotions bouncing around inside me, I decided to remodel the kitchen in my house. I am not sure where it came from, but over the years I'd become a home remodeler and furniture maker. My dad said I got it from my great-grandfather, a person I'd never met. In a way, when he said this, it made me feel invalidated, like I couldn't have possibly just developed these "manly" skills on my own. But another part of me liked the idea of skills being passed down through genetics.

Usually when people ask me how I learned how to do home remodeling, I reply, "I just watched a YouTube video." But perhaps there is something deeper there. While I do not even have any memory of my grandfathers, they both passed away when I was two years old, I wonder what my great-grandfather would think of his skills being passed down to me. Since I can't have kids, I wonder how he would feel knowing that the passing of that skill stops with me.

I didn't do much with carpentry prior to my transition. In middle school, I carved out a piece of wood to resemble a race car, even though it looked more like something used in a fertility ritual. Its bulbous head thinned into a shaft before expanding in the back to make room for me to rout a hole for a CO_2 cartridge. The cartridge was meant to power the cars so that we could all race our creations to see who made the best aerodynamic vehicle. After applying blue paint to my piece of wood, I set it down with the others to dry.

The next class, we all set our cars down on the linoleum floor of our woodshop and then crouched down with a pin in our hands, pins that would be pressed into the CO_2 cartridge. A loud pop came from all the cars and they began to move across the floor. My car sputtered a foot or two, others kept buzzing across the room. While I don't think I was last place, I definitely was not first, second, third, or even seventh.

The following week in woodshop, we learned how to build a small tabletop bookshelf. While slightly lopsided, mine still sits in my basement, gathering dust. Lastly, I learned how to press multiple blocks of wood together and then spin them on a machine called a lathe. As the square block of pressed wood spun around, I used a sharp tool that was slightly larger than a flat-head screwdriver and slowly whittled the block into a curved wood bowl. It now holds my extra change, when I have it.

Those skills in middle-school woodshop and instructional design were the extent of my work with anything that would be considered carpentry. After my transition, and buying my first house, I started to purchase tools and practiced home improvement by drywalling, resurfacing wood floors, and laying down flooring. I did this partly because I didn't have much money, so I couldn't afford to pay someone to help. I also did it as a hobby and a way to make me feel more connected to my male identity.

As a kid, I would be right next to my dad helping him build a platform for an old pump that used to pull water from the ground on his parents' homestead in Kansas. Now it was a garden decoration. I dug holes with him to plant trees and new fencing to separate our pasture from our grass. I loved every minute of it, and now I loved going into the hardware stores and buying tools and supplies by myself. I liked wearing my leather boots and jeans with tears in them and stains on the fabric. I liked having a pencil behind my ear and a tape measure clipped to the waistband of my jeans. It made me feel like a "man."

I grew up in the decade where the TV show *Home Improvement* was on in a large number of households. We would all laugh at Tim Allen's character, who was all about being a "man," but was actually quite inept at everything. While I was taught that men fix things, from watching the show we saw how hyper-masculinity often failed. The more refined sidekick, astute neighbor, and wife and mother of three were the ones that actually carried and saved the patriarch of the family.

△

When I moved in with Lily, it was my first experience being in an Arts and Crafts home from the early 1900s. Sadly, over the past one hundred years, the home had been in the hands of people who didn't know the art of décor or remodeling. Our kitchen was one of those victims. What should have been a large open space, with deep-brown woods, Victorian tiles, and high ceilings, was a room squashed by a drop-panel ceiling with halogen lights, like what you would see in an office cubicle. The open room was cut off by a large white Formica kitchen island, with an uneven cabinet perched above, held only by an exposed four-by-four piece of wood from the hardware store. There were tiles on the floor that I can only describe as being nipple pink. To try and offset the terrible colors, Lily had painted the walls a bright yellow. The yellow was a good choice, but the rest was terrible.

At night, while sleeping, I could feel our home's soul quietly crying to us, *"Help me."* I believed that the occasional water leak from one of the cardboard ceiling panels was most likely the house physically crying. For over a year, I would mentally take notes about things I would like to change. In the mornings before having to start work, I would run searches on my computer on what kitchens looked like in that style home back in the early 1900s. I then began to figure out how I could keep it period-appropriate, while also functional in modern times. I had originally wanted to wait until my speaking season slowed down, and for the summer to begin, before the deconstruction and reconstruction process. However, with all of the emotions bouncing around in me surrounding Karen's declining health, I needed a release. I decided it was time for my kitchen to no longer quietly whimper at night.

The nipple-pink tiles that lined the floor were the first things that needed to go. The tool for the job was a five-pound hammer that I had named Thor. I first ran an angle grinder (a handheld tool with a small metal disc attached to it that spins) on one of the grout lines. The hardened surface was grinded away, opening gaps between each tile. Dust quickly entered the air and coated everything in the room, including my full body. The mess was part of the fun to me; for Lily, not so much.

Next I took Thor, along with a crowbar, and began popping the tiles off the floor. I could feel my hand vibrate with the first hit of the hammer against the metal of the crowbar. The vibrations ran through my hands' bones, all the way up through my elbows. It was somewhat uncomfortable, but it also made me feel alive. I took another swing. A piece of the tile broke off and flew toward my face. Fortunately, I was wearing goggles to protect my eyes from any random shard of porcelain tile, but my cheeks had a few flecks of crusted blood from the tiniest of dislodged pieces.

I didn't let pain, or a little blood, slow me down. I kept whacking, as hard as I could. Images of Karen's face, images of her ailing body, a body that had now lost its hair, kept entering into my vision. My eyesight became fogged as tears began to stream from my ducts, only to get caught by the plastic of the safety goggles pressed against my cheeks.

Behind me, a pair of little eyes watched with confusion, along with curiosity. The eyes belonged to the bravest of my four pets. The newest member of the family, a cat we named Newt after a character in Lily's favorite book, *Lonesome Dove,* let out a meow and then leaped over me. He landed onto the white Formica counter. He hunkered down onto his haunches, pleased to be perched with a better vantage point. I remained squatted in a catcher's position, swinging my right arm up and down frantically. Sounds of tile breaking and flinging around the room echoed through the space.

"Fuck you, cancer," I repeated, swing after swing. Finally a sharp throb in my elbow signaled that it was time to take a break. I released my catcher squat position and leaned my butt against the heels of my feet. After dropping my hammer and crowbar, I lifted the safety goggles from my face. It was the first time that I took in my progress. As the dust from broken tiles and grinded grout settled, I saw a square space the size of a large cardboard box cleared. Where the tile used to be, there was now aged and worn yellow vinyl flooring from the 1950s. Below that was the original pine floor filled with nails to keep it from creaking. I had hoped to refinish the original wood floors, but they were too damaged to re-sand and stain.

I looked up toward the ceiling. I had removed the ceiling panel, which had been stained by the mysterious water leak, allowing me now to see the original nine-foot expanse. The drop ceiling had only given us seven feet of space. Taking a look around the rest of the room, I thought about its history, and wondered if other people were propelled to create change through sadness.

It took me another three days to fully chip out the old floor. By the end, my elbows were too sore to move, and my hands could barely squeeze a bottle of shampoo when I showered away the debris from the destruction. I imagined how Karen felt with the chemo, and how her soul would feel when it knew it was time to leave her physical body.

CHAPTER 11

BLUEPRINT FOR MOURNING

Selfie 106 – March 2014

The day that I was supposed to unscrew and remove the white cabinets and tear out the Formica counter had to be put on hold. Instead, I was in my car, driving an hour west to the city of Lincoln. My phone was perched on my leg, with Google navigation running.

"Your destination is to your right." I turned on my blinker and pulled into a large parking lot, which was already filling up with cars. "You have arrived at your destination."

I turned off the navigation so that I wouldn't have to hear the annoying robotic voice reminding me of my arrival. I then turned off the key to the ignition. In front of me was a large brick building that created a mini skyline of four towers, the one in the middle being the biggest. I took in a deep breath before opening my door and beginning the lonely walk into the Catholic church, where Karen's funeral was being held. In the middle of the ceremony, the priest read a testament I had written about her.

"'I know her energy and love will live on in all of us who have been touched by her.'" It sounded strange to hear his low voice read what I had posted on my social media regarding Karen's passing. At the end of the sermon, when the robed men walked down the aisle with their metal cages swinging back and forth from chains, releasing the smell of frankincense, I believed that I could feel Karen's spirit there with us, a congregation hall that was filled to the brim.

⚠

While sensing her presence in the church was calming, my sadness and anger followed me home and into the rest of the year. Karen had been like a mom to me. Every time something exciting happened in my life, I would share it with her, knowing she would be proud, which, in turn, made me proud to make her proud. She was also a dear friend to me, confiding in me with her worries about her kids, her feelings about losing her mom at a young age due to breast cancer, and her concerns for the future.

A piece of me left this earth when she did. More specifically, a piece of my accountability around my eating disorder recovery left this earth when she did. When my eating disorder became full-blown as a teenager, it was during a time that I felt lost, confused, sad, and alone. While I had many people around me as an adult, unexpected deaths can bring back the same feelings. During my time of grieving, awareness or feelings around hunger went out the window, along with all the kitchen debris I was clearing from my path. I didn't want to eat. I could feel my pants getting looser, so I had to start wearing a belt, which I kept tightening. The shoulder and bicep region of my T-shirts were no longer clinging to my muscles. All I wanted to do was work on my house, and if I did feel hunger, I would drink a couple beers. I didn't drink to get drunk, or to the point of passing out. I just found it to be more satiating than food, plus food required chewing.

My unhealthy behaviors reminded me of a time Karen confronted me back when I was still in graduate school. Her scolding took place one afternoon at the health center where we both worked. I shared an office with another grad student named Julie. While at first, I did not like Julie—I didn't want to share my office space—we quickly became best friends. "My office" became "our office," a space that contained me, a newly out lesbian (not aware of my transgender identity yet), and Julie, the person responsible for me coming out. To break up the monotony of working in a small room situated in the basement of our campus health center, during our lunch breaks we started the tradition of walking off campus and over to a coffee shop. (Incidentally, this was where I had spent many hours over seven years writing short stories while drinking coffee and puffing on cigarettes.)

The coffee shop was a perfect college hangout. It was L-shaped, with the top of the L being designated as the smoker's section. Julie and I would light up cigarettes and take puffs in between a bite of our hummus wraps and giant cookies. This had become our ritual. One afternoon after returning from our lunch outing, Karen had walked into our office to go over a document I had created for Eating Disorders Awareness Week. She stood behind me, looking over my shoulder at my computer screen. Suddenly I felt her breath on my head. She was sniffing my hair, which at that time I wore shoulder length. I knew I had been caught.

"Have you been smoking?!" She was exasperated.

I slowly turned around and looked up at her, embarrassed and ashamed. "Yes ..."

Julie's back was to us, her long blond hair shifted as she proceeded to hunch her shoulders and lean her head down closer to her computer screen. Her fingers typed away on her keyboard, acting like she didn't hear our conversation.

"I can't believe you! You could get cancer!" Her mom voice was noted. She stomped out of my office. I knew she was disappointed. Even after her reaction, I continued to go on my lunch outings with my friend, but I felt guiltier each time I returned.

After her funeral, I had this memory, and instead of feeling guilty, I felt pissed off. There she was, a nutritionist with a balanced diet and exercise routine, yet she still died from cancer. Then there was me, a survivor of the eating disorder that has the highest mortality rate of any mental illness, a person who used to smoke (but not inhale), and yet I was still here.

Cancer is not fair.

△

Life in and of itself is unfair because no matter a person's religious or spiritual beliefs regarding what happens after we die, the one thing we all do know is that we die. The body of a person we know stops and does not return to us. Having now faced the fourteenth death of someone I cared for in my life, I started to think about life and wondered how long I would make it on this planet. Two of my biggest emotions when thinking about death are sadness and fear. I worked long and hard to get to where I am, and I now have a life partner that I want to explore this world and life with, so I don't want it to end.

When I first started my transition, my brother voiced his concern for my heart health due to the weekly testosterone injections. Yes, testosterone does lower good cholesterol levels and raises bad cholesterol levels, which are contributing factors to heart disease. However, I personally am more concerned with heart disease being caused by stress and anxiety, not testosterone injections. Studies are showing that hormone therapy is a safe and effective long-term medication. While there are risks with anything, if patients use the medication as prescribed and follow other guidelines (not smoking, eating a balanced diet, and integrating exercise), the risks are lower. Any potential risks of a shortened life due to my transition do not concern me; I couldn't have lived much longer on this planet without the transition. What does concern me is how this world treats trans bodies and the voices that come through them.

When Lily and I talk about death, I tell her that I am going first. Statistically, I will most likely die first, but when I say this, I realize that I am being selfish and also weak. Being without her would be too hard, but how will she feel? Since we don't have kids, who will take care of her? I can understand why people hold religion or spirituality close to their hearts; the realities that come with life are hard to think about and accept.

△

The day I cleaned off the haze left from the gray grout, which I had pushed into my black metal backsplash, signaled the end of the kitchen remodel project. The pink-nipple tile floors were now a dark oak wood. The yellow walls were now a midtone green called "Grandma's Linens." The white Formica countertops were now dark gray cement blocks. The panel ceiling was now gone, so were the halogen lights. The kitchen turned out beautiful, a room built from hands full of sorrow. It was a room that brought me some peace when I stood in it. In looking back, I find it fitting that the room I chose to remodel as a result of Karen's illness was the kitchen. This was a room where we cooked and ate meals, a room that allowed us to nurture and bring nutrition into our bodies.

CHAPTER 12

THE POWER OF FAMILY TIES

Selfie 133 – June 2016

Two years after Karen's death, I still fought the overwhelming feelings of despair that I experienced knowing she wasn't reachable anymore. I—again—questioned the point of life, the point of trying so hard, only to pass away and become a blip that is eventually forgotten. As I began to question the point of my own mortality, it made me scared for my parents. In the past, my eating disorder was too hard for them to watch, or for us all to face. In the present, we were all watching each other change, due to the effects of aging. I knew that in another twenty years my parents could be gone. I didn't want to look back at my life and have regrets about not spending more time with them before they leave this planet. Having them at my wedding was our first step toward reconnecting, but that was a onetime event (at least I hope).

I knew it was time for me to make more of an effort that went beyond special events. Looking over my calendar one morning, I noticed that I was scheduled to speak at a conference in a town near my parents. In the past, I would not mention my engagements near them, nor make the time to see them. Now I decided it was time for a change. I picked up my phone and found my parents' number in my contacts.

I heard my mom's voice answer: "Hello?" She always sounded a little confused when she answered the phone.

"Hey, Mom!"

"Oh . . . hi!" she responded back.

I wondered what it was like for her to hear my voice now. I wondered if she even remembered what my voice sounded like before my transition.

"I am going to be driving past Aurora on my way to a speaking engagement in a couple of weeks . . . which made me think of you."

"Oh!" She laughed.

"Would you like to have breakfast with us?" I heard my dad's distant voice come through the receiver. Whenever I talked to them on the phone, my mom would be the person holding the phone, and my dad would selectively listen in on the conversation. I would forget that he was in the room until I heard his muffled voice chime in from time to time. I had to laugh at this because I realized I did the same thing when people called both Lily and me.

Genetics are a wonder, connecting our souls even when apart. I also find gender to be a wonder. While we can pick up different characteristics from our parents, regardless of gender, the connection and characteristics that I shared with both my brother and my dad linked us to something deeply rooted within nature, not nurture.

"Yes, that would be nice," I replied.

"Well," my dad's voice paused. "We'll only have some toast and jam."

I knew he was kidding. If there was one thing my parents loved to do, it was feed other people. Most memories from my childhood revolved around meals at either our kitchen or dining-room table. I could only imagine how frustrating it was for my parents when I became sick with anorexia and didn't want to take part in the daily ritual where they felt most nurturing. While my transition had pushed us apart, my eating disorder was the wedge that broke the surface.

△

Although my parents still lived in the town I grew up in, they had moved to a new home. When I pulled up to their house and stepped out of my car, I could smell the bacon on the grill and fresh bread, buttered and crisping, on the griddle. I walked up the four stairs that led me to the front door of their ranch home. I opened the screen door, and then the front door, without bothering to knock or ring the doorbell. I knew the door would be unlocked; it was one of the charms of living in small towns.

While the home itself felt like a stranger, the aromas and furnishings sparked memories from my childhood. As I closed the door, my ears were greeted by the ticktock of the grandfather clock. I couldn't think of a memory in my life where that clock wasn't in my parents' home or standing in the background of a photograph of us children before leaving the house for formal events. I walked past the swinging pendulum and around the corner into their formal dining room, which had a long cabinet separating it from their kitchen.

As I got closer to the cabinet, I softly questioned, "Helloo. . . ?"

As the words left my mouth, I rounded the corner and saw my mom whirling eggs in a bowl. *I guess we'll be having scrambled eggs today,* I thought. The way she stood in the kitchen was the same way as when I had watched her cook when I was a kid. She always looked down at what she was doing with intensity. Her eyes wide open, her upper teeth biting her lower lip, which was curled upward in a smile. I missed being a child and feeling that secure space in that moment.

She looked up from the bowl. "Oh! Hey!" she said happily. She dropped the wooden spoon, which was in her hand, and walked over to me. Both of our arms wrapped around each other. I wondered what it felt like for her to wrap her arms around my shoulders now versus when my body was still ruled by estrogen.

Did I feel more familiar to her back then? Do I feel more happy to her now?

For me, wrapping my arms around her was always the same. I felt big. That day, it was an okay *big* feeling. My mom had always been a small-framed person; at age seventy, she was even smaller. While her body size had changed, her face—minus the wrinkles—was still the same mom I had seen as I was growing up.

"Oh, hey, kid!" my dad said as he walked in from the back porch. On his hand was a hot pad, he was definitely grilling the bacon. I walked up to my dad and gave him a bigger hug than I had in the past. His body was very similar to when he was younger. While also being smaller and a little bonier, his shoulders still felt broad.

I was proud of the way my parents took care of their health by staying active. Their favorite activity was walking; actually, I wouldn't describe it as walking. I should refer to it as trotting that looked deceitfully like a walk. As a child, I learned that my legs had to move every millisecond when out with them; otherwise, I would be left behind in the dust. Today, when people complain about how fast I walk, I say, "Blame my parents."

115

At seventy, they still went out on their trots, stopping only if my mom saw flowers that she liked or a bird that was worth gazing at for a birdwatcher.

"Well, I think everything is ready," my mom said as she looked at her griddle and stove. "Let's grab our plates and sit down."

I looked over to the kitchen table. It was the same table we all sat around when I was sick with my eating disorder. When I sat down, memories rushed into my mind of how stressful it was in the past when we were scooted around that brown tabletop. Sitting in front of the spread now, I found myself going back to my old anxious habit. My right-index finger shot up over my right eyebrow, where it began to rub the skin, back and forth. While that was a common reaction when I was nineteen and struggling with eating, it was something I hadn't done as an adult, except now. Muscle memory is powerful; it has its own form of consciousness.

I let my right hand drop from my forehead and started to reach for my fork, when a phone rang. I watched as my dad got up and walked over to an old secretary desk, where they stashed their random everyday items, mail, keys, and now a cell phone. I was expecting to see him open up a flip phone. They usually made jokes about still being in the Dark Ages because of their old technology. Instead, I saw a large rectangle in a black-and-blue silicone case.

"We upgraded," he said while he tilted his head up and directed his eyes down toward the phone, as if he were looking through bifocals. As long as I could remember, he had always worn trifocals, making him naturally adjust his head to see different distances through his glasses. After having cataract surgery, he no longer needed trifocals. It was his own form of muscle memory. He glanced at the caller ID and set the phone back down.

I sat there, with my mouth open. I never thought the day would come when my parents would upgrade their technology to be with the cool kids.

"They have classes for us on how to use one of those things at the community center in Florida," my mom said, referring to their snowbird home.

"That's really great! I'm proud of you both." With the flip phone, my parents had told me not to text them because it costs ten cents. With the flip phone, I couldn't call them except after seven p.m. because that was when they wouldn't get charged for calls. I hated talking on the phone, to have to remember (and be motivated) to call them after seven meant I never called. The introduction of the smartphone was a whole new ball game for them, and for me.

After breakfast, my mom stood up and started to clear the table.

"I can help you with that, Mom," I said, not wanting to be the stereotypical male who made the women clean up after a meal.

"No, it's all right. I'll only be a second. You can sit here and talk with your dad."

It is so weird how quickly people can change expectations of you based on presentation and gender roles. If I was still female-bodied, I know my mom would have looked at me and said, "Well, I guess *we* should clear the dishes."

⚠

Even at family gatherings, I would now watch as my sister helped my mom with meal prep and table settings. As a kid, I would have thought I was being sneaky and getting away with something because I wasn't in the kitchen with the rest of the women. Now I felt guilty and lazy.

But I knew that if I asked my mom and my sister, "Do you want me to help with anything," they would reply, "No, no, we got this. Go and give your father some company."

So, with their prompting, I would then proceed to the fridge, grab one of my dad's Budweisers, and stand out in front of the grill with him. Minutes would slowly pass as we sipped on our beers and talked about the well-groomed grass and how long the meat had been slowly searing on the top rack.

The way we are socialized in society based upon gender is definitely an interesting one—and one where I am grateful I have been on both sides of the fences. It helps me understand the challenges and barriers we have created.

⚠

After my mom left with the dishes, my dad and I sat in silence.

"That HB whatever thing in North Carolina is ridiculous," my dad said. He was referring to a law passed in North Carolina called HB2, or House Bill 2, which stated that transgender people must use the restroom based on whatever gender marker they had on their birth certificate. If not, they were breaking the law.

I looked at him, in shock. When I was a kid, my dad would randomly bring up politics. I'd hear him grumble about the Clintons and give praise to the great president Dwight Eisenhower. Anything else he said, I let go through one ear and out the other. As an adult, we never talked politics, abiding by the rule that one should never talk about politics or religion. I guess my dad decided it was time to drop that rule.

"People should just be able to use whatever restroom they want," he said while shaking his head.

We didn't make eye contact at that moment, but I knew an olive branch had just been extended toward me. His comments were a sign that he was opening up his heart to transgender people. I felt that his comments were also an invitation for me to start sharing more about my trans identity and my work.

△

Later that month, I was in New York City walking in between the skyscrapers near Times Square. I was in a suit and didn't want to break a sweat, so my usual quick pace was slowed down to a nice stroll. In one hour, I would be providing a keynote speech to a large financial firm. Knowing that my dad had a smartphone, I decided to test the waters further by first taking a selfie of myself mixed in with the skyscrapers and then texting it to him. It was always awkward, at least for me, to take a selfie in public, especially when people were walking past. I felt like it read "tourist," "narcissist," or "lonely guy who doesn't have anyone to take a photo of him." To try and counter my own embarrassment around people, who most likely were not even paying attention to me, I acted like I was not actually taking a photo.

The picture I snapped showed the left side of my face while I looked off into the distance, the large skyscrapers towered over my body. I looked like a businessman in my light gray suit jacket, blue-and-white-checkered shirt, and a red plaid tie. The pose conveyed, *Look at me!*

Small-town boy doing grown-up things in the big city. I added the photo to a text message and hit the send button before sticking the phone back into my pocket.

Allowing technology to break down the data that made up my selfie, in order to send it to my dad's phone, I continued on with my evening. I walked through the large glass doors and entered the building where I would soon be sharing vulnerable aspects of my life with complete strangers who were part of Corporate America. While I waited for my contact person to escort me to the room where the event would be held, I turned my cell phone to airplane mode. It was bad enough when other people's phones interrupted one of my talks—having my phone do it was worse.

After the engagement ended, I arrived back at my hotel and turned my phone back on. It immediately began to vibrate with different notifications, one of which was a text from my dad. I opened it up and read: *Don't hurt your neck looking up at all those skyscrapers. You look great, I love your tie.*

The glow of my screen highlighted the smile that I had running from ear to ear. All I could think was *Wow*. Like at my wedding, when my mom told me how nice I looked, my dad just complimented me on my appearance. Not only how I looked, but how he liked my tie. When I was a kid, I had a gray dress that I liked to wear to church on Sunday, not because of the dress, but because its accessory was a pink tie. But, hey, guys can wear pink! The kids at my church would tease me when I wore this outfit. "Only *boys* wear ties," they would say as they circled around me, sneers on their faces. I felt ashamed and insecure, so I quit wearing my favorite Sunday outfit.

Now, at age thirty-six, I felt liberated from those insecure feelings through approval from my father. I also felt excited to have a new way to communicate with my parents that would work for both of us. I hated talking on the phone because I couldn't hear, and my dad, who had worked road construction to get him through college, also hated talking on the phone for the same reason. But we both, I learned, liked to text. Writing was an easier way for us to form our thoughts and share our feelings. When I was in college, we would always e-mail one another. Those e-mails had stopped after my transition, which essentially ended our communication with each other, until now.

△

A week before my thirty-seventh birthday, two months after my first selfie was sent to my dad, he took a page from my playbook when he texted me a picture of their RV set up at a camp spot. Since it seemed so random, I began to wonder if he accidentally sent the picture to me instead of someone else.

Nice camp spot, I wrote. *Where are you?*

I watched as the three dots bounced and waited for his reply.

At Haworth Park in Bellevue.

Dad! That is right next to me! We should get together.

How about we take you out for dinner for your birthday?

In the last ten years, I had only spent one other birthday with them. Some birthdays I would receive a phone call, others would be recognized with a generic card, and some had passed completely unacknowledged. I'll never fully understand how my parents operate. It could be something explored endlessly in therapy with no real answers, so I try not to think too deeply about it. I naturally chose a brew pub for my birthday dinner. A good birthday to me equaled having good beer.

The server placed us at a table that was tucked away in a corner, but not tucked away from the voices of the other bar patrons. I couldn't even remember the last time I had been to a restaurant with my parents. However, I took note that if we were to go out again, I needed to choose a location that was a little less popular. Trying to hold a conversation with aging parents in a loud bar was like trying to have a conversation in English with a person who only spoke French. Our conversation gravitated to what was natural for us, surface conversations that wouldn't make anyone uncomfortable. We could have not said anything at all and I would have still been happy just looking at their faces. Their different facial expressions brought up memories from our past together, while also providing me with insight of how I, too, will change as I age.

After we had finished our meal, the server placed a paper box that contained half my sandwich in front of me. My parents had decided to split a sandwich; too much food in the evening prevented my dad from being able to sleep well. As we stood up to leave, my mom looked at me and said, "I want a picture with you."

You want a picture with me? I thought. This question may sound silly to some people, but no matter what actions they take, there will forever be a small part of me that questions whether my parents can fully accept my transition.

"I'll take a photo of the two of you," my dad said before pulling out the smartphone. With a press of a button, he captured me standing with my arm wrapped around my mom's small shoulders, hers around my waist. We were both close to the same heights, but I appeared slightly shorter due to leaning my head, covered by a sweat-stained ball cap, so that I was touching her. It was a picture that could have been taken year after year, a mother with her son.

"I'll text it to you," my dad said. Those were still words I wasn't used to hearing him say. As I drove them back to their car, my dad sat next to me in the passenger seat. Unprompted, he said, "People today do not understand transgender people." He paused, then said, "They are just people. Like anyone else!"

I about slammed on my brakes. Fortunately, the desire to prevent a ten-car pileup on one of the busiest streets in my city prevented me from moving forward with the urge.

"And you know what? There are LGBT people in our senior-citizen community in Florida and people ask us what we think about that. All I have to say is 'Who cares!' Two of the guys there are my best friends. We go on walks and play tennis together . . . And you know how we feel about the Clintons, but we *hate* Trump, so we're going to vote for Hillary."

I continued driving as my dad talked, questioning if I had driven through some alternate universe portal, and wishing I could pinch myself to see if everything I was hearing was real. I wanted to hug my dad right then, but I kept my hands on the steering wheel and let his words serve as the hug until I was able to come to a full stop. My seventy-year-old parents were different from my fifty- or sixty-year-old parents. Time and patience can create change. If we allow ourselves to open up our hearts and look past labels and judgments, we all can change. When I pulled up to their truck, we all got out.

"Thank you again for coming out and for dinner," I said as I hugged my dad.

"It was really nice. Happy birthday," he said back.

I went over to my mom and gave her a long hug. "Thank you for supporting Hillary."

My mom started to chuckle. Politics was something we still weren't talking about with one another.

"You are voting for your kid when you vote for her." I released the hug and took a step back. At that moment, I became sad for people who refuse to change. I feel bad for families that fall apart and are never able to reassemble, even if in just small pieces. The history contained in families, both during our lives on this planet and our links to our ancestors, was something I never wanted to lose.

"I love you both very much."

"We love you, too," my mom said. I released our hug and watched as she got up into their truck. She smiled at me before closing the door. That night, they would return to their RV at a small campground; the next day, they would begin their drive to a home and life in Florida that I still had not experienced, but had hoped to do so at some point.

The next day, I went onto social media and sent my dad a friend's request. He had been on the platform for at least a year, but I had ignored the "People you may know" notifications with his picture, until now. In a way, it felt silly to even think that sending my own father a friend request would solidify us as having a relationship, especially since I held an ever-growing disdain for social media. Yet, when I saw that he was "friends" with my other family members, in that moment it mattered to me to have the two of us also connected.

A week later, the request was accepted.

CHAPTER 13

FINDING "SELF" ON THE OTHER SIDE OF THE MOUNTAIN

Selfie 135 – August 2016

For people with facial hair, it usually happens in your late thirties. First one gray hair pops through on the underside of your chin. Then another one pokes through in your mustache. Before you know it, your beard is graying like the muzzle on an old dog. The changing in hair color is a sign of aging, another reminder of our mortality. I was reminded of my own mortality while standing at the top of a mountain pass, looking over the Sierra Madre mountain range stretching north from Colorado into the southwestern region of Wyoming.

As the sun rose, its rays slipped over the mountains' ridges, extending orange and yellow light into the valleys, from the dark shadows. While taking in the beauty and gaining my breath from a climb that would put any gym stair-climber to shame, I began to think about how amazing it was to be out in the middle of nature and away from any civilization. No sign of cars, no air or noise pollution, no other humans—unless the day before, they, too, had hiked ten miles and climbed four thousand feet in elevation with thirty-five-pound packs strapped onto their backs. Standing there, engulfed by nature, I felt so small, but also so large, in the world.

What is today? I thought. *Tuesday. Today is Tuesday . . . OH! Today is my birthday!* I couldn't believe I had forgotten what was supposed to be *my* celebratory day.

As a child, I would spend days before my birthday feeling giddy. Birthday cards with one- or five-dollar bills from aunts and uncles would start to arrive in the mailbox. Bags of unopened jelly beans and chocolate began to appear in the cupboard, a sign that my mom was getting ready to make a cake from scratch. After it mostly cooled, she would then smear the cake with homemade vanilla frosting before adorning it with all of the delicious morsels of pure sugar.

On the official day, her creation would then be revealed to me and everyone else as they all sang "Happy Birthday." I would eagerly watch her slowly walk from the kitchen into the living room, her face and moving lips illuminated by the lit candles on top of the candy-laden treat. After scarfing down my corner piece chock-full of delicious goodness, I would then excitedly tear the paper off boxes containing new shoes or sports gear.

Now, with each birthday, I would get excited by people buying me a beer, after I had finished shopping with the 15 percent birthday coupon that had been sent to me in the mail by a retail store. Being in the mountains, with no beer or retail stores around, the anniversary of the day I was born could have easily slipped by without fanfare or recognition. Suddenly my feelings of both being sad and relieved by how irrelevant an actual birthday could be was interrupted by the sounds of heavy breathing and the clicking of aluminum poles on top of loose rock. I looked over to my right and saw Lily's head slowly ascend from below the ridgeline, behind her was her very sweaty father. Their backs were weighted down by full packs that heavily bounced with each of their steps.

"Phew!" Lily exhaled.

"That was a little rough, first thing in the morning." Mike's breathy voice came from over Lily's shoulder.

"Oh, wow!" Lily added as they both joined me and looked out over the ridge. Besides the sound of them catching their breath, we all stood in silence.

"Today is my birthday," I said while looking at Lily and Mike.

They both looked confused at first, then stunned, and then a little ashamed. "Oh," they said in unison. "Happy birthday. . . !"

At that point, we had all been up for well over three hours. In that time span, we had first wriggled out of our sleeping bags and climbed out from our warm tents into the frigid and slightly damp morning. We then gathered our water from a lake, by hand-pumping the murky liquid through a filter. We trekked the water over to a lit camp stove so that we could use it to drink our instant coffee and choke down oatmeal mixed with raisins and chocolate. After breakfast, we changed into our hiking clothes, which held the stench and slight dampness left over from yesterday's climb, before breaking down our campsite and stuffing everything back into our bags.

During those three hours, there had been no birthday song or simple acknowledgment that I was officially a year older. I decided that I wasn't mad that they forgot, even though I did take a mental note that I would never let them forget that they forgot.

Lily walked closer to me. I could tell by the way she slightly lifted the right corner of her mouth that she felt like the worst person in the world, forgetting the birthday of a person she had been with for six years and had been married to for four. I also knew her eyes were most likely a little squinted, but that way of showing her shame was hidden behind her sunglasses, which were shaded by the visor of the Superman ball cap she wore. Looking at the ball cap, I felt a rise in my blood pressure.

That was my Superman ball cap, I thought. But I couldn't hold on to the anger long. Lily looked good in that hat. She looked even better in the hat while standing in the mountains. She leaned over and gave me a small kiss. I could taste the salt from her sweat mixed in with mine. We then stood there, looking at what we could see of each other's dirty faces as the sun continued to rise.

The excitement I felt, doing something I loved with the person I loved, could have been used as her get-out-of-jail-free card, but she couldn't seize that opportunity. It was at that moment that she decided to point out the first gray hair to ever appear in my beard.

"Oh . . . you have a gray hair right there." She pointed at the hair on the left side of my face right above my chin.

"Come on!" I said jokingly, while internally shouting, *Fuck!* The hairs on my head had been graying since I was eighteen, but being notified that my beard was also starting to shift was not exactly the present I was looking for that day.

At least the views in front of me were nice. It was also nice to be out doing something I had let slip away from me, due first to my eating disorder, and then to my transition. Being out in the mountains on my birthday felt like a rebirth of parts of me I had lost, parts that move beyond gender.

I fell in love with backpacking when I was nineteen years old. In college, you have the opportunity to get one college credit each semester through "fun" classes. After completing weight-lifting class during my sophomore year, I began to plan my junior-year class schedule. While scanning through the booklet, I saw a backpacking class listed and immediately highlighted it in blue. The first day of class I took a seat in the front row and eagerly waited to learn about how to survive out in the wilderness. My notebook quickly filled with my scribbled handwriting on what to do in extreme weather, how to use a compass, and how to read squiggled lines and different shading on a flat piece of glossy paper called a topographic map.

During the class where the instructor had us unfold our maps and place a compass on top of the lines that designated the different levels of elevation, I was taken back into the pages of one of my favorite childhood books. *My Side of the Mountain* was about a young boy who ran away from his home in New York City so that he could live in the woods and survive off the land. He taught himself how to hunt so that he could eat, how to stay warm by tanning the hides of what he killed, and how to stay protected by sheltering himself inside a hollowed-out tree. To keep from becoming lonely, he stole a baby falcon from its mother's nest and then trained him.

I read the book four times over the course of one summer and acted out what I read in the trees behind our country home. The canopy provided by a large pine tree became my hollowed-out shelter. The birds that perched on the tree limbs and looked at me before chirping and flying away became my falcon. While the boy in the book fled the city, I was able to flee my insecurities. The body I lived in became gender free, because there was no one else around me to invoke the need for having a gender. In my imagination, I flourished.

As an adult living in the real world, the further my physical body was integrated with civilization, the more I lost the ability to find solace in the wilderness. Confined within a dorm room, placed within the limits of a city that was foreign to me, my new solace had become physical starvation. I had lost touch with nature; the backpacking class provided the embers to rekindle a feeling of freedom. When the class instructor informed us that we would be taking a weekend trip in a state park as our class final, the fire inside me became reignited.

As I hiked with the class of twelve students up and down the muddy trails, more memories from my childhood book rushed over me. The more I pushed myself, the less I thought about gender or appearance. All that mattered was how I would handle each step ahead of me. It felt freeing to be doing an activity where nothing was defined, and there was room for error. If we missed a turn, or if we became too tired, our shelter, bedding, food, clothes, and even entertainment were strapped right there, onto our backs. The only time on the trail where I was even reminded of gender was when I had to use the restroom. Squatting in the forest is not a fun experience and no matter how you try to angle it, you will get some urine somewhere on your feet, calves, shins, or inner legs.

When the sun's rays became blocked by the fall foliage still clinging to the trees and the moon's pale beams started to peek through the opening of the limbs, it was time to go to sleep. At least for me. My eating disorder began before my sophomore year; so being malnourished for over a year, I was starting to severely feel its physical and mental toll. That night, as I lay in my sleeping bag, I ran my hands over my protruding hip bones to gauge how much weight I thought I might have lost that day. I still experienced a rush of endorphins when my body burned the energy, now reserves, contained under my tight skin.

This is one reason anorexia is so sneaky; the high you first feel is addictive. What's also addictive are the glances you get validating that your physical changes fit into a desired ideal. Yet, the thinner you become, the high you feel and the glances you receive begin to change. At that point, though, you don't know how to stop. I knew the other students on the trip were disapprovingly looking at my thin face and arms, which were all bones and elbows. I could no longer squeak by under the radar of being "super fit." Being covered by my sleeping bag provided me with a shield from what I assumed people thought about me. The cool material comforted me as I tried to focus on the sounds of the cicadas' chirping buzz, instead of the sounds of my growling stomach.

When I returned from the weekend trip, I stepped onto the creaky metal scale in the female locker room at the gym. My body had indeed dropped more weight. My brain wanted more, while my tired bones wanted rest. Regardless of how physically tired I was, something was shifting within me. The fantasies of living in the wilderness from my childhood were being joined with the reality of my adult experiences. I knew that I wanted to be in nature where I could keep my body moving, and flee my insecurities, but I couldn't live my life as a hermit. I knew that I needed some form of human connection. Being part of outdoor adventures would be a way for me to have both. Sadly, the weekend trip officially ended the backpacking class; one credit would soon be added to my cumulative score.

The day I walked to our campus recreation center to drop off my class-issued backpack, I felt like I was losing something I had just found. I begrudgingly pulled open the door that led into the outdoor-rental portion of the recreation center. Concrete floors and walls contained a space full of backpacks, sleeping bags, skis and poles, life jackets, camp stoves, climbing ropes, and more. All of it screamed new adventures, new ways of using my body while also not being alone. I walked up to the metal counter and set the green-and-black bag on top. No one greeted me, so I briefly thought about walking back out with my bag. But I knew that would be considered stealing, so I decided to summon a staff person by banging on the tiny bell next to the cash register.

As the *ting* of the bell echoed off the concrete walls, I looked around and noticed a large bulletin board next to the counter. It was covered by different-colored flyers. Most were flyers announcing upcoming climbing, backpacking, or white-water rafting trips; others sought roommates, which I assumed were placed there by the student staff. As I heard someone's footsteps approaching me, I found my eyes zooming in on a flyer for a job posting. Underneath the announcement in large block letters, I read, OUTDOOR ADVENTURES IS HIRING! BECOME AN OUTDOOR LEADER WHILE LEARNING WILDERNESS SKILLS. I felt a rush of hope surge through my heart. Below the posting was a job application. I snatched it from the board and clutched it in my hands. The application was due following Thanksgiving break, and interviews would be taking place during finals week. I had to say good-bye to my backpack that day, but I hoped we would be reunited in the very near future.

⚠

The feeling a person has when riding down a large hill at a comfortably high speed on a bicycle was the same feeling I had when I zipped up my newly issued black fleece with the title *Outdoor Trip Leader* embroidered over the left chest pocket. I was entering into the second semester of my junior year of college as somebody with a purpose. I was no longer just a student. I was no longer just the eating disorder patient. I was Kim, a trip leader with Outdoor Adventures.

I soon learned that the downside of having a community meant that people actually noticed you and had a name to go with noticing you. Among my fellow outdoor-adventure and campus-recreation staff, I was not that "thin" or "skinny" girl. We all had an intimate connection. I could tell by their glances that they were concerned by my dwindling figure, and I quickly became self-conscious while feeling embarrassed and ashamed. I didn't want people to see me, but the more I worked in life to make myself invisible, the more visible I became.

I decided that I needed to change in order to fit in better with my peers. I needed to be stronger and have more energy, in order to start moving up the ranks among the other wilderness leaders. Like when I was a student on the high-school basketball team, I never wanted to be on the junior varsity team, or a benchwarmer on the varsity team. No, I wanted to be a key score-leading player. Starving myself wouldn't get me "off the bench" in this new challenge, so I explored how I could gain strength and weight without having my brain freak out. To do this, I first had to reframe looking at eating food as a way to build muscle. If muscle was on my body, I would be okay.

In order to help ease my anxiety around putting on weight, I found myself watching a girl at the gym. Her body was strong and big, while her body-fat percentage was low. I noticed that she lived in my dorm and that we were on the same eating schedule, so I would wait for her to arrive at the cafeteria and then sneakily get in the line a few students behind her. Each scoop of food she took, I also took. Along with increasing what I ate, I also started taking supplements: protein shakes, protein bars, and creatine powder.

My body slowly started to change. Over the course of the semester, glances started to shift away from concern. In fact, they started to shift away completely. While people around me were pleased with the physical changes they saw, I became more and more misanthropic. What I thought would be my cure, my way of feeling like I fit into society, was only a mirage. I soon started to believe that my childhood fantasies and adult realities could not be combined in a way that connected me to something in life.

As I entered into my senior year at college, the growing discontent that I felt in my physical body and my eating disordered brain started to become a problem on our trips. Especially when the hiking for the day had ended and the evening meals were set in front of us. My brain kept casting full and curvy images of a female body in front of me with each bite that I took. I tried to hide my anxiety by slowly chewing my potatoes or noodles and then swallowing without letting other people see all I wanted to do was throw up. I couldn't let people know what I was feeling.

I kept shifting my thoughts away from my body and onto my role. As a trip leader, I was clad in my official fleece and my hiked-up wool socks, which were contained within beat-up leather hiking boots. I had hoped this outfit would define my identity. Clothes had always been used as my armor, a way to prevent people from looking past the fabric and seeing a person and, more specifically, a gender. My uniform gave me confidence and defined me as a trip leader whose job, regardless of gender, was to safely guide inexperienced people in the wilderness. This was not easy to do.

Our trips were always scouted, meaning completed, by a couple of staff members prior to taking our patrons out into the field. The scouts would create a trip plan with total miles hiked, elevation gains and losses, camping spots for each night, and how to circumvent challenges like an eroded trail or a missing bridge across a raging river. The problem with trip planning is that it was impossible to plan everything out. From the unknowns of the wilderness and the weather, you also had to work with guiding inexperienced hikers with varying personalities and abilities in your group.

I quickly learned that many people who sign up for outdoor adventure trips love the idea of backpacking, but when put to the test, they were not mentally or physically prepared for the reality of what they were doing. While taking a group of college students on a six-day trip into the belly of the Grand Canyon, we had one girl reciting a verse in the Bible about walking through a valley of death, another crying about the weight in her pack, and another guy who wandered off in the darkness, whom we fortunately found.

On a different trip, another leader and I took Girl Scouts, aged thirteen to sixteen, to a small mountain range in Wyoming. We had to first abandon the actual backpacking part of the trip because the complaining and crying kept growing with each step they took. Fortunately, after a mile, we reached a campground where we set up camp for the next two nights. Our backpacking trip officially switched to day hiking. During our lunch break at one of the many lakes, the girls started to hop around on the rocks sticking up out of the water. With each hop they took, I noticed an increasing desire to splash around.

"Can we *puh-leasse* take our boots off?" they asked while looking at me with puppy-dog eyes.

"No. I don't want you to hurt yourselves," I said.

"Ah! But look! That girl has *her* shoes off!" Four of the six girls pointed at a young woman standing fifty feet from shore on top of a rock. She was waving at what I assumed were her parents and siblings standing shoreline.

"Sorry. No," I said again.

The girls continued to slowly hop from rock to rock. In between each rock hop, they would look up at the young woman, sigh, and then look down to skip again. All of us turned and looked over to the young woman when we heard a scream and large splash. She was no longer standing on the rock; now she was submerged from shoulder down in the ice-cold lake. We heard her laughing as the group she was with continued to stand there, watching. Then her laughter turned into a bloodcurdling scream. The rock she had been standing on was a broken piece of sharp slate. When she slipped, her foot was like cheese pressed against a knife; her arch had sliced open, down to the bone. My girls looked at the blood in the water with horror on their faces.

My co-leader went into the water to carry the young woman to shore as I ran toward them with our emergency bag in tow. We first secured her bloody foot inside her shoe to put pressure on the bleeding before calling an ambulance and establishing an evacuation plan. I led the girls down the trail as my co-leader assisted with bringing the young woman down the mountain's path. As we walked, I tried to point out different types of flowers to get the girls' minds off the incident, and to keep myself from saying, "See, I told you so." There is a reason why the "wilderness" is called that—it truly is *wild* and *unpredictable*.

The unpredictability kept my negative thoughts briefly at bay, but they didn't remain silent. My thoughts about my body and how alien I felt in it were becoming too much. This became apparent to me after a trip we completed for a group of sixty Girl Scouts. The trip took place in the summer, which in Nebraska meant it was hot, humid, and sticky. Our base camp was situated in the Sandhills, which are exactly as they sound. These are hills of compact sand held in place by a thick covering of prairie grass that is home to cattle, prairie dogs, and snakes.

The camp was abutted to a field that had cattle grazing the tall and thin grass. We quickly learned that this field and the cows contained within the wood and chain-link fences were part of a research project on the digestion process of different grass in the cows' four-chambered stomachs. What this meant was there were portals that went from the outside of the cow into their stomachs so that researchers could reach in and grab samples . . . it was just as gross as it sounds.

When the first group of young girls, eager for an adventure, started to step off their bus, you could see the expression on their faces quickly shift from excitement to disgust. In front of where the buses stopped, twenty green tents were sitting on top of searing hot ground. Along with the tents, they could see large and flat piles of dehydrated cow pies, most likely left by the sci-fi cows. Smoke rose on the east side of the compound from the chicken breasts searing on top of a cast-iron rack that was attached to a large fire pit. As the juices from the meat dripped, flies flitted from cow pie, to chicken breast, to cow, and repeat. To keep the girls from evaluating the scene too deeply, each of the nine leaders grabbed a group and escorted them to their tents. As we helped them with their sleeping bags and mats, we started to ask questions to learn more about their personalities and who would be best paired in a canoe going down a river together the next morning.

While serving dinner, we noticed one girl didn't touch her food. Her brown hair hung over her face in straggled strands. Her arms were thin, and she moved as if walking through Jell-O. The next morning, she didn't touch her breakfast. Then lunch came, and she took two bites of her sandwich. Alarm bells started to sound. That evening before dinner, we found her passed out. She had taken Benadryl, which was considered contraband. It was at that moment we decided to have a staff person take her back home, ending her time at the camp.

I had never felt more useless than I did on that trip. I couldn't help this girl who was clearly struggling with anorexia nervosa. As she walked by me that night on her way to the van, I tried to make eye contact. I had hoped, by looking at me, she could tell that *I was one*, like her, but she barely glanced at me. Instead, she dipped her head lower and let her straggly hair cover her face. My boss held her arm to stabilize her as she climbed up into the passenger side of the green van. She kept her eyes averted down as she buckled herself into her seat, while another staff person closed the van's door.

I kept hoping she would look at me once through the dusty window to see that there was hope, but I knew that my eating disorder had officially become one of many identities hidden below the surface. I wasn't emaciated; in fact, I had gained a lot of weight at that point in my recovery. My face was puffy, and my stomach was round from the creatine and other supplements I was consuming. While in the past, being a trip leader helped save me from my eating disorder, the more time I spent in recovery, the less connected I felt with myself and my body.

The canoe trip took place the summer before I entered into graduate school. My depression was growing, along with my anxiety. I decided, for my own mental health and for safety reasons, to submit my resignation letter as a trip leader. Not fully ready to let go, I asked to be moved from the field to behind the checkout counter of the rental shop. With some of the pressure off me, I started to shift my focus to graduate school and understanding more about myself. While this was the best decision, it decreased my wilderness trips to once a year while in college.

After graduating and starting my transition, my trips became nonexistent. My adventurous spirit became lost. I was too busy focusing on my newfound transgender identity and on the bodily changes that I underwent week after week. I didn't have time for the outdoors; instead, I worked. I needed money, not fun. Fun wouldn't pay for the different medical procedures that I felt I needed to join my internal spirit with my external shell. For the next fifteen years, my backpacking equipment sat in large plastic bins in my basement. I would occasionally glance at everything and sigh as I mourned for the different pieces of my past that once meant so much to me.

△

I reconnected with my adventurous spirit on a whim. My unknown travels were ignited when Dylan, a younger trans man from Seattle, e-mailed me to let me know that he was going to be doing a summer internship in Kansas. We had been in communication over the years, mostly through e-mail exchanges about my experience with having lower surgery completed in Belgrade, Serbia. We then met in person when he and his wife attended one of my sessions at a transgender health conference. When I received an e-mail from him asking if he could spend a weekend with us over the Fourth of July while he was in the area, I didn't hesitate to say yes. Transgender identities can link you like family, even if you barely know one another.

While we sat outside on our patio and waited for dinner to finish on the grill, he mentioned that he would be car camping all the way back up to Seattle in two weeks. Hearing the word "camping" brought all of my memories of the wilderness rushing over me. My heart pace began to quicken with the thought of being back out in nature. Lily and I spent a lot of time hiking, but we always returned to a bed that sat under a roof with air-conditioning and a shower.

"My sister camped with me on the way down . . . I'll be doing the trip back up, all alone," he said.

"Maybe I should come with you," I blurted out. It felt weird to be so impulsive about something that would take me away for almost two weeks, in just two short weeks. Especially since I barely knew the person who would be my car and camping companion.

Dylan's sharp, but soft, green eyes looked at me. His lips were pressed together as he nodded. "Maybe you should," he said.

The next thing I knew, I was tossing my backpack, which had been gathering dust for fifteen years, into the back of his fully packed car before heading north to South Dakota. The next eight days, red dashes on a map of the US traversed across Wyoming, Montana, Idaho, and coming to a stopping point in Seattle. On this trip, we hiked, white-water rafted, rode horses along the mountainside, and jumped into rivers from cliffs. Each day ended with a hot meal cooked over a campfire as we held cold beers in our hands. It was a time where I felt "manly," not because of the activities—I did all of these things before my transition—but because I had found a friend who defined and encompassed life as a man the same way I did. I related to him through kindness, compassion, patience, and respect—while also having far too much fun building the perfect fire in the fire pit.

The next year, I flew out to Seattle and we spent five days on the Pacific Crest Trail. When I returned home, I was like a child at show-and-tell, flipping through the pictures I had taken, while talking about jumping into cold glacier lakes and watching a herd of elk roaming between the tree line and the water with their calves. I could tell that the more detail I shared, the more envious Lily became. She voiced her desire to try something she wasn't sure she could physically do: "I want to go there. I want to see that. I wish I could do that ..."

⚠

When Lily stood alongside me on top of the ridgeline in Mount Zirkel Wilderness, she had proven that she might not always remember my birthday, but she could climb a mountain with a pack on her back. She didn't know then, but on that trip, she had given me one of my best birthday presents ever. I had been trying to get her to backpack with me for a couple years, but each time I suggested it, she would become frustrated and say, "I can't. I'm not strong enough." When I heard her say that, it made me aware of another way socialization had impacted her beliefs around her female body and its abilities. By pushing past her fear that she couldn't physically complete a backpacking trip, she discovered how much she loved it. I loved being able to guide her on these trips and teach her about how to navigate the wilderness trails and rugged landscape.

Now, with each birthday, we cross off more than a week on our calendars to go out together into the secluded and vast mountain ranges. Doing this with my best friend, my wife, is the ultimate birthday gift that will never expire, break, or be left forgotten on a shelf or in a closet. We always return from trips, beat up but feeling recharged . . . that is, until we think about having to go back to work and logging onto the online world. My anxiety instantly grows when I take my cell phone off airplane mode and the vibrations of e-mails and text messages start flooding my notification screen. When this happens, I yearn for turning my Jeep around and driving back into seclusion. However, I know that Lily and I both still have work to do, and fights to battle for humanity.

I try to reframe the way I look at this world through what I learned while on a backpacking trip, since each trip presented new challenges for me and my own fears. When we are hiking along a ridgeline where there is over a thousand-foot elevation drop on one or both sides, I tell myself, *Don't be anxious, don't think about falling. Just put one foot in front of the other and have confidence in yourself.*

When I return home, I remind myself that confidence is what allows me to keep putting one foot in front of the other, even when the fear I am facing are other people, not the unknowns of the wilderness and their tricky trails. Sometimes I do a better job of reintegration, other times I struggle a bit more with how to handle my work as an advocate while also being an imperfect human being.

PART THREE

CONFIDENCE:
STORIES OF FACING FEAR AND FACING MYSELF

It is always awkward when you begin therapy with someone. As you walk slowly behind the therapist, toward the office door, you realize that in a few seconds you will be entering a room and sharing stuff about your life that you may not want to really talk about. Stuff that maybe even the people closest to you don't know. It can feel dirty at times. It can feel shameful. It can feel downright raw. Especially, when tears begin to unexpectedly stream down your face.

—Ryan K. Sallans

CHAPTER 14

HITTING MY SECOND ROCK BOTTOM

Selfie 140 – December 2016

There is nothing more depressing than a waiting room. Sure, some may argue that there are plenty of things more depressing: abandoned puppies and kittens stuck in cages on the TV commercials that ask for money, the obituaries, or the current way we elect presidents in the United States. But when you are sitting in a waiting room, depressed, knowing the reason you are there is to see a therapist, then nothing else wins.

It had been almost twelve years since I'd seen a therapist, minus a few sessions. I tend not to count those because in my last session, when I was talking about my negative body image, the male therapist proceeded to have me take my index and middle finger on my right hand and begin to methodically tap my left wrist. He then instructed me to follow his lead and repeat what he said.

"I am a good person." Still tapping my wrist.

Then tapping my chest. "I like my body."

Move to tapping under my eye. "My body is good to me."

Next I am tapping underneath my armpit. "My body is healthy."

We repeated the whole mantra, three . . . more . . . times.

It was the longest four minutes of my life. My heart rate increased and sweat began to seep out of every pore in my body, causing the back of my shirt to stick to the leather couch. All I could do was think, *This is the most ridiculous thing I've ever done.*

I vowed at that point that I didn't need therapy anymore; I just needed to step up and be aware of my feelings. Over the next three years, I reluctantly recognized that my feelings were getting lost. Lost in my work. Lost in the online world. Lost in beer and Netflix binges. Even trying to write creatively, I was lost in surface words. My brain couldn't take me to places of magic or memories of happiness. Every time I tried to start a chapter, it began with the same three themes: *Life is so dark. The online world sucks. I feel so alone.*

Frustrated, I began searching for those feelings of being alive and sought out moments of inspiration through watching TV. Hearing and seeing characters go through different life struggles in movies and shows always helped me unwedge my own emotions that got stuck within my body. Like when I was a child watching a movie where I saw a character transform from a girl to a boy simply by wishing on a star, it gave me hope.

This time, my depression was so deep that hope wasn't exactly what I was searching for; pain and sadness felt more appropriate. I quickly became obsessed with the movie *Into the Wild.* While it had been out for several years, I had never seen or heard about the story. The movie was based on the true story of an affluent young man who graduated from a prestigious college, gave away all of his money, and then drifted from town to town before going to Alaska to live off the land. *Spoiler alert*: He died of starvation in the wilderness.

I discovered that, along with the movie, there was also a book written by Jon Krakauer, so I went out and purchased it, even though I already knew the ending. I then discovered that Eddie Vedder is a music god and downloaded the whole movie soundtrack. After a month of rewatching the film and listening to the soundtrack over and over, I decided it was time to watch something more uplifting.

Of course, I was depressed; so more uplifting equaled a movie about a young woman struggling with anorexia, to the point where she might die. In this movie, *To the Bone*, she voluntarily discharged herself from the New Age recovery center, where she had been staying with other teens and young adults. The film psychologist, played by Keanu Reeves, was confronted by the girl's mother. When she asked why he would let her daughter go, the therapist said, "Recovery happens when people hit rock bottom. In treatment centers, we intervene before they can do this because it is too hard to watch." The female character with anorexia was heading to her bottom. *Spoiler alert*: She did not die at the end.

A memory started to replay as if I were having an outer-body experience. My present self was standing there, watching my anorexic female self lying on the floor of my dorm room. I was nineteen years old and ready to die. As my breathing slowed and my heart pace quickened, then stopped, then heavily beat again, I heard an inner voice say, *"It's not your time to go."* Within a millisecond, I jumped up off the floor, called my parents, and stated that I would seriously begin my recovery from my eating disorder.

Now, twenty years later, I was sitting in a different room, in a different city, but with the same voice pleading with me to take that millisecond to make a change—a change that will dramatically shift the trajectory of my life with just one choice. While I had hit rock bottom with anorexia when I was nineteen years old, at age thirty-six I was feeling a new wave coming if I didn't start to do something about it. As the film's credits were rolling, I looked at my watch. It was six-thirty at night, too late for a professional to answer the phone. I searched for the phone number of the therapist that both Lily and I saw when we were going through the stalking. I liked her strength, humor, and no-bullshit approach. She reminded me of Karen. I knew she would push me to explore the feelings I was trying to drown. After hearing her voice mail's greeting, I said, "I need to see you. I just need some maintenance work."

A week later, I was sitting in her waiting room, mixed in with the obligatory office chairs, all mismatched. I decided that I preferred them over chairs that were so matched you felt that they should scoot up to a dinner table. The silence in the room was interrupted by a large bang that rattled my ears, followed by a slow and drawn-out squeal. As heat began entering the room, I realized the noise was coming from an old radiator under the window. On top of the radiator sat a pile of magazines with corners bent and pages stuck up in different directions. It seemed like a bit of a safety hazard, but I didn't want to touch them. I could only imagine how many hands had touched those pages, how many germs had been spread across Jennifer Aniston's ridiculously airbrushed face in the Aveeno lotion ads, how many sneezes were captured by the pages as people read about celebrities exiting rehab.

Everything about the waiting room roared the word "displacement." To try and escape from how uncomfortable I felt, I searched through my jacket pocket for my phone. As the screen glowed, and my thumb started to make an upward motion to scroll through nonsense news, I found myself laughing. This was one of the reasons I was there, to figure out a way to get away from the online world, especially when I was feeling uncomfortable. I tossed my phone back in my pocket and began to take in some deep breaths. Fortunately, no one else was in there with me, so I wasn't embarrassed to practice breathing that sounded a bit like Darth Vader before he announced that he was Luke's father.

"Hey there, you ready?" I heard the voice of a woman from the doorway. I looked up to see the person who would become my new therapist.

"I guess so," I responded as I stood up and started to exit the room of displacement.

It is always awkward when you begin therapy with someone. As you walk slowly behind the therapist, toward the office door, you realize that in a few seconds you will be entering a room and sharing stuff about your life that you may not want to really talk about. Stuff that maybe even the people closest to you don't know. It can feel dirty at times. It can feel shameful. It can feel downright raw. Especially, when tears begin to unexpectedly stream down your face.

"It's good to see you," my therapist said as we both sat in our respective places. Hers was a large, comfy chair; mine, a small couch that didn't invite *too* much comfort.

"It's good to see you, too," I replied. Even though it felt awkward to say that, since I was there due to feeling like a worthless imposter in my own community.

"What do you want to talk about today?" She placed a legal notepad on her lap and crossed her legs. I wanted to tell her that she shouldn't use a notepad. It disrupts the connection and intimacy of a therapist/patient relationship, but I refrained. I knew that thought was just me trying to keep my own barrier up, so that I didn't have to talk about the hard stuff. So instead, I looked at her long hair, which framed her smooth yet sassy-looking face. Her presence made me feel somewhat relaxed and trusting. Thinking about the therapists that I have seen, I realized I did better working with women in their fifties and sixties. They reminded me of my mother when she was younger. They made me feel more open to being nurtured.

"I don't know . . ." My classic response. A knee-jerk reaction to the emotions I held hostage through mental shutdowns. "I called you the other night because I feel stuck . . . I feel anxious . . ."

"Okay, you feel stuck. What does 'stuck' look like?"

It was a question that had my thoughts twirling in my mind. Words moved from left to right across my vision. As I reached out to grab them, they vanished into the smoky whirlwind, making me have to wait until they came back around again, if they even would. My silence was the physical demonstration of exactly what stuck felt like: speechless, scared, confused, disappointed, and disenabled.

The work I do, assisting people in moving from a place of intolerance to acceptance surrounding the lesbian, gay, bisexual, and transgender community, is tiring. Most people think it would be tiring from the ignorance in the room—the "dumb" or "offensive" questions that people ask—but those are the moments that I love to be in. If I was educating a room full of people who knew everything and knew all the "right language" to use, there would be no reason for me to be doing this work. What actually wore me down were the people of any identity who felt entitled to tell me how I should be doing my work based on what *they* think is important, or the folks who hate me because of a headline, a photo, or because I could no longer be what it was that they wanted or needed. While sitting there, blankly looking at my therapist, things that people had said to me started repeating slowly in my mind. As they repeated, my throat started to tighten, and the pace of my heart increased.

"*Ugh, I can't believe you said the word 'FTM.' That is soooo outdated. Soooo offensive.*" My experience: FTM refers to female-to-male, which was, and can still be, a term that is used by transgender men. Today, a more common term is trans man, but guys may switch between the two.

"*How dare they ask about how they do a surgery! They can just google that.*" My take: While asking a specific person about specific body parts or surgery is offensive, and should not be done without invitation from the trans person, many people are curious about how bodies can be changed through surgery. If a person doesn't want to talk about it, it is fine to say that the asker can google that. But as a transgender health educator, I personally like to assist people in understanding transgender medicine.

"You are heteronormative and reinforce the binary, so you don't matter." My feelings: Being transgender is extremely complex and should not be discounted by writing a transgender person off as being heteronormative (meaning they are promoting a heterosexual life view of a man being partnered with a woman) or reinforcing the binary (meaning a trans man presents his gender in a more hyper-masculine way and a trans woman presents her gender in a more hyper-feminine way). For many people who are transgender, the transition is meant to get them to a place where they are seen by society as the person they've always felt they were internally. We all have the right to present our gender in a way that is comfortable and authentic for ourselves.

The judgment and assumptions that spill out of some individuals' mouths or (more accurately) from their keyboards makes me want to stand up on top of a mountain with a megaphone and shout, "I understand you are hurting. I understand you are angry. I understand there are ridiculous injustices happening. BUT when we fight against each other, judge each other, and shut down ANY opportunities for people to seek education and language, we are only further marginalizing and polarizing the cause." I wanted to speak up, but the online world had me feeling like a deer in headlights. So instead, I turned toward attacking myself, while falling into a deeper depression.

This depression leads to avoidance. In the past, I avoided feelings through starvation; now I avoided feelings through beer. I could feel my body temperature rising as I tried to find the courage to state this realization to the patient woman sitting across from me. As the clock ticked in her office, I could tell she was studying my body language and facial expressions. I kept starting to speak a sentence, but then hesitated. As my chest thumped with my increasing heart rate, I weakly said, *"Stuck* . . . is me watching Netflix and drinking too much beer at night." It was now out there, even if it was just in the tiny ten-by-ten-foot space of her office. It was out there. There was a witness.

Images started running through my mind showing people's judging eyes. People's disgust and disappointment in Ryan Sallans, the role model and reputable speaker in transgender health care. I could hear people saying, "Ryan Sallans should know better." I was starting to feel like I was morphing into my own role model, Superman (played by Christopher Reeve), in the third movie of the 1980s franchise. In this movie, his character turned bad after being exposed to lab-made Kryptonite.

When I was a kid, I found this movie upsetting. I didn't like his slouched posture and his mean voice. I didn't understand why he flew to Italy to straighten the Leaning Tower of Pisa before flying over to blow out the Olympic torch as it lingered over the wick, preventing the runner from being able to light the flame. I didn't like seeing him sit at a bar and drink whiskey while flicking nuts at the bottles of liquor lined up behind the bartender, breaking them and spilling the contents.

As an adult, I have found a new appreciation for the metaphor behind these scenes. His character slipped from perfection, and this slip made him human. Me drinking more than the daily-recommended allowance of alcohol had become my own Kryptonite, making me feel broken. In the movie, the young son of Lana Lang yelled, "Superman, you're just in a slump!" I felt like I was in the worst slump of my life. I was embarrassed and ashamed. I looked up toward my therapist, expecting to see the same judgment.

She looked at me and said, "Oh, that's not good. How much are you drinking?"

"When I am not traveling for work . . . three to four a night. . . ," I lied. They say in health care to always double whatever a patient tells you if they drink often. When I used to go into a doctor's office, I would say I drank a couple beers a day, which meant four (four was accurate). Now upping it to three or four, I knew that she knew that number was more likely six to eight.

"Okay. Your assignment is to start thinking of other things you can do at night instead of drinking beer and watching TV."

"Okay," I said. Even though in my mind, I couldn't visualize an evening without beer. I used it as my medication to stop, or at least quiet, the anxious voices in my head. I knew that even bringing up drinking was deflecting from the deeper issues that left me paralyzed, but I didn't want to talk about my feelings. Instead, I played the same game that I did with my eating disorder therapist from college. I stalled by stuffing down my feelings and averting the conversation until our fifty minutes were finally up.

I left therapy that day thinking, *Why can't I just be okay with . . . me? Why do I keep living in fear and negativity?*

Instead of actually sitting in the discomfort to answer that question, I again diverted my thinking about the rest of my day. I knew, no matter how hard I would try to resist, once I started to get anxious about the online world, my job, or writing, I would walk over to my fridge and pull on the stainless-steel handle. Then I would reach over to the left-hand side, where I always organized my beer cans by brand. My hand would come out with a cool aluminum can containing a delicious and hoppy India pale ale. I knew that I would then walk out of my kitchen, around the corner, and into my den, where I would plop my body on the worn green couch. (My wife, Lily, had informed me multiple times that I'm color blind and that the couch is actually the color taupe. I say I just see color on a large spectrum.)

After kicking off my cowboy boots, I would place my feet on top of our leather ottoman, turn on the TV, and crack open the top. I would then sip away, all while getting lost in the characters in front of me. I had gone from being the person who used restrictive eating as a way to try and control my discomfort, to a person taking in large amounts of calories through a substance that had no nutritional value. What it did have, however, was an exceptional numbing value.

That night, while the glow of my TV comforted me, along with my beer, I realized that my next challenge in life was tackling my relationship with alcohol by revisiting my relationship with myself—not as a trans man, not as a public figure, just me as a human being. The home alarm system in my house beeped and then a woman's robotic voice sounded from the speaker, "Back door." Lily had arrived home from work. I heard her first greet the excited miniature dachshunds, who had waited for her, and then heard keys drop on the counter followed by footsteps.

As she rounded the corner to greet me, I saw a big smile on her face.

"How did it go?" she asked. I could tell that she was proud of me for going to therapy. She had wanted me to go for years.

"Fine" was all I said. I glanced into her dark brown eyes. She looked disappointed, but not surprised by my one-word answer. I could tell she was frustrated with me, six years together and I had become the stereotypical male who drank beer, said few words, and rarely shared emotions. I no longer wanted to feel numb or portray a stereotype. It was time for me to finally start moving forward in my emotional journey. To move forward, I knew I needed to deal with the complexities and influences of the online and external world's perception of me as a man.

As she walked back to the kitchen, I remained staring into the other room. On the wall were three frames that contained pictures from our wedding. I thought back to that day and to all the major events that have happened in my life because of my transition. I thought back to all the students asking me questions with the hope that I had the answers they were seeking. I thought back to all the talks I gave corporations, universities, and health care facilities, educating tens of thousands of people on how to be better employers, providers, and educators.

Thinking about all of the places I have traveled over the past fifteen years, I realized how the energy in a room shifts when we tell a story. While we all do have different identities, we can still connect with what it felt like when we fell in love, lost someone close to us, been mistreated by an employer, or heard our parents say, "I love you." It was time for me to yell, "Ryan! You are not a label, damn it!"

As humans, we are not good or bad; we are complex and seek anything that can make us feel connected. So it was time for me to reframe how I was experiencing the world and take pride in what it was I did best: being vulnerable and then using my voice to share what I have learned through storytelling. Doing this allows individuals in an audience to process their own feelings and understanding of life more deeply.

Photo by Fred Schneider

CHAPTER 15

MAKE AMERICA GREAT A . . .

Selfie 143 – March 2017

Oh, isn't that cute, he's wearing a shirt from that TV show Stranger Things, I thought . . . or rather wanted to believe. I was standing near the entrance of a room, located in the middle of a Student Union in Texas. In twenty minutes, I would be giving a talk about my transition to an audience composed of students, faculty, and community members. The room was set up classroom style; chairs were lined up, row by row, all facing a large projection screen.

On the screen was an image of myself in a white T-shirt, black golfer cap, and duct tape across my mouth. The tape had been gently affixed to my lips so that it wouldn't rip off my facial hair when removed. A temporary tattoo had been pressed onto the left side of my cheek. In black capital letters was the word **NO** and directly underneath were the joined letter and number **H8**. The photo had been taken by Adam Bouska, a famous photographer from the *No Hate Campaign*. I felt the image was appropriate to use as a title screen, a subtle message for respect.

Minus when I was protested by the Westboro Baptist Church, the evening had begun like any other event. That was, until three young men passed through the propped-open doors. I could only assume they were first-year students at the university. Their faces were in between teenage and adulthood; strong hairlines on wrinkleless foreheads, smooth cheeks that only required shaving every few days, and a smattering of acne— signposts induced by a puberty that started most likely six years ago.

I felt my posture straighten as I made eye contact with the first man in the group. I then took an unconscious step back, providing me more distance from his energy and the feeling of acid being blasted onto my skin through his glare. He continued to promenade past me in his gym shorts and knee-high socks tucked into dirty sneakers that were unlaced; the other two men hesitantly followed behind. It was clear who the alpha was, the most dominant of the three. I was trying hard not to form my opinion about them based on their appearances, but doing this work for as long as I had, guys like them didn't attend my events unless it was mandatory, which this was not.

I found myself forgetting to greet new people entering the room. Instead, I watched the three men who had now walked past the back row of chairs, moving closer to the front. Curious people who attended my events, but who also were uncomfortable, typically sat in the back row. The trio bypassing that seating section made me further nervous about what had motivated them to join us.

I then noticed that on the back of the leader's shirt was a 1980 presidential campaign logo for Reagan and Bush. The logo was the same one I had recently seen on an episode of *Stranger Things*. Only, on the show, the campaign logo was seen on yard signs that were strewn across the neighborhood in the fictitious town. Several scenes in the program showed heroic children frantically riding their bicycles past the signs as they were either riding away from danger or heading into a battle with one of the demons from the "upside-down world."

My thoughts continued to race: *Maybe one of them is trans. Maybe they are just curious. Maybe they want to learn something.*

I was wrong.

I realized this after walking up to the front of the room to join the organizer for the event. Student volunteers closed the doors in the back to reduce any noise from the hallways. We both stood there and surveyed the medium-sized crowd. She then leaned down to my ear with her head still turned out toward the audience. In her Southern accent, she softly said, "It looks like our friend has a new accessory." I followed the direction of her nod and found myself moving past the first two rows of heads and landing on a very bright red hat . . . then I read the lettering *Make America Great Again.*

"Oh, that's nice," I said while attempting to suppress the feelings of rage that overcame my body every time I saw that extremely misguided phrase that propelled a presidential election. *Man, I can't escape that damn hat today,* I thought while thinking back to my flight to Texas. While washing my hands in the men's restroom at my connecting flight's airport, an older man loudly asked, "Is it hot in here? Man, I'm hot." I looked at his reflection in the mirror and saw that he was wearing a MAGA hat.

I wanted to respond by saying, "It's probably because of that fucking hat you are wearing." But I resisted. I remembered one of my own experiences where I was wearing a shirt from Obama's 2008 presidential campaign while walking through a hardware store. A middle-aged man wearing a camouflage jacket looked at me and my shirt, and then said in passing, "Obama? What the fuck!" His statement rattled me and made me forget why I was even in the store that day.

While standing there looking at the old guy's red hat in the restroom, I remembered how I felt in the hardware store, so I decided to quietly exit the room and find the gate for my next flight. Some people may point a finger at me and say, "By remaining silent, you are part of the problem." My response to this would be to ask them to gently lower their finger and take a moment to move outside their own ego. What that phrase means to me is hate, denial of women, minority and LGBTQ rights, support for white supremacy, and . . . a second round of hate. What that phrase means for the wearer may be very different.

Whenever I see anything that goes against my political views, from bumper stickers to T-shirts, to those stupid red hats with white lettering, I take a breath and remind myself that their proponents would feel the same way about my own bumper stickers and T-shirts. Their life experiences and beliefs are different from mine, and by shouting at them, it only reinforces their need to become louder and angrier at me and my own beliefs and values. We don't see change when people remain in a defensive place; change happens when we are able to find a way to slowly lower our guarded walls. This requires maturity, patience, compassion, and the willingness to be uncomfortable with one another.

It took strength for me to stand in front of the hat and the unknowns, but it was my job as a professional to remain composed. I turned my attention back to the other audience members and began to scan all of the faces. I liked to use the energy in a room to help guide my own comfort and sense of safety. In this situation, I felt a huge sinkhole, three rows back, and to the left. In front of this sinkhole were two rows of students, many of them members of the LGBTQ organization on campus. While the red hat with offensive lettering sat behind them, they all wore their rainbow buttons or shirts with blue, pink, and white lines running across, a symbol for transgender pride. I was thankful to have them closest to me. I was thankful that they didn't see the hat unless they turned around, but I couldn't imagine them not feeling the searing glares burning through the backs of their necks.

"Should we get started?" the organizer asked.

"Yeah," I said, anxious to see where the night went. I watched as she grabbed the microphone. It was then that I noticed it wasn't a wireless handheld microphone, but one that was plugged into the sound system, tethering me to the left side of the room, where the podium was located and the three men sat.

The organizer tapped a few times on the wire mesh to make sure the microphone was on, and to grab everyone's attention. The small chatter that had been bouncing around came to a slow hush. "Thank you, everyone, for coming to this event tonight. I also want to thank our Dean of Students for being here." She pointed toward the back of the room. Everyone followed her hand and nodded to acknowledge the dean's attendance. The organizer then finished with her introduction and handed me the microphone. Before she left my side, she leaned down and whispered, "I pointed out that the dean was here to encourage all students to behave."

"Thank you," I whispered, before clearing my throat. "I want to thank everyone for taking time out of your busy schedules to attend this event tonight. As I share my story with all of you, I ask that we respect one another. There is enough hate in the world. We don't need to reinforce it in this room tonight." I didn't usually open with that line, but I felt it was needed to further keep the unknown actions of the young men in check.

As I moved forward with my talk, I kept finding my vision focusing in on the third row, left side. It was impossible not to look at the leader's face, drawn long and tight, jaw jutting out and stiff. His dark eyes followed every move that I made. Each time I tried to position it so that a student in front of him blocked our shared line of vision, he aggressively shifted his body left or right while leaning farther forward. I knew that he wanted to make it clear that he was watching me and that I couldn't escape.

I grew tired of this game, tired of feeling uncomfortable and having my talk lack in spirit because of him, so I decided to use the words "penis" and "lesbian" as often as I could. This decision came after talking about sexuality and using the word "penis" for the first time that night. As the word flowed off my lips, the young man sitting in the middle of the three nearly jumped out of his seat before grabbing the leader's arm and shaking it. They both then began bouncing up and down like monkeys in a cage while their mouths formed into shocked O shapes. I couldn't believe the simple two-syllable word would get such a reaction from two out of the three hecklers.

The third young man had chosen to sit at the end of the row. He remained very quiet. His eyes were gentle, along with his body language. As I described the differences between sexual orientation and gender identity, I could see the wheels in his brain turning. There was hope for him. He reminded me of me, when I was a freshman in college.

⚠

The political and social landscapes were extremely different in the late 1990s and early 2000s. The Internet was still in its early years, social media was nonexistent, and cell phones were plastic devices with numbers that were actual buttons and had tiny screens. It is weird to think back and realize that I didn't even own a cell phone until I entered into graduate school. When it came time for me to be eligible to vote, I registered as Republican. Not because I had any real deep thoughts about politics and my feelings around social issues, but because I didn't know anything different. I grew up in a town where the majority of people were Republicans, and those who weren't remained silent.

I'm ashamed to admit that at age eighteen, when I voted in my first presidential election, I voted for George W. Bush because I didn't like Al Gore's wife's name, Tipper. My views and exploration of politics and their impact on social and environmental issues changed as I entered into graduate school and I saw how politics impacted everything around me, including my own identities. This would be an accurate way to describe privilege. Because of my race, socio-economic status, and immaturity in life, I didn't experience nor was aware of the injustices that impacted other people on a daily basis.

I could only assume that the three men sitting in the room that night, who were around age eighteen, also identified as Republican. This political affiliation isn't necessarily a bad thing . . . unless their view of being a Republican is denying any human being civil rights and . . . well . . . anything associated with the phrase "Make America Great Again." I know that several presidents have used variations on that phrase, including Reagan, George H. W. Bush, and Bill Clinton, but what exactly does "great again" encompass? For many people, including myself, it is a phrase that *royally* flips off racial and social justice. That night, as I looked at the three men who supported MAGA, I felt the silent one at the end of the row could possibly shift his views and politics, like I had, in time.

⚠

As I continued to speak, my microphone began to cut in and out. I tried to ignore it and proceeded to shift from speaking about language and terminology to my own personal story. When I shared a story about my long strawberry-blond hair that my mom would aggressively brush, braid, and then pin up, making it look like I had honey buns affixed to either side of my head, students in the first two rows began to laugh. As laughter rolled from their chests, MAGA scooted his body closer and started to make jeering and exaggerated breath-filled cawing near their ears, mocking their excitement and engagement.

Should I ask them to leave? I pondered.

I looked at the students in front of them. They still had smiles on their faces; their body language showed they were relaxed. *Not yet,* I decided.

Finally the microphone I was using completely failed. I set it down, and while we waited for tech support to bring a new one, I spoke by loudly projecting my voice. Out of twelve years of speaking in front of audiences, I was amazed by how uncomfortable I felt by this one eighteen-year-old student. Besides the shifting of his body, the mocking of other students' laughter, and the uncomfortable stares, he was behaving. He wasn't holding up signs, interrupting me, or doing anything else to bring attention to himself, but there was something about him, something about his political clothing choices. The saying "Make America Great Again" rattled me greatly. I became saddened by how our political affiliations are moving us to a place of hating one another.

The doors to the back of the room opened and two men in white polo shirts and khaki pants scuttled to the front. My body literally sighed when I saw that in one of their hands was a wireless handheld microphone. I quickly grabbed it and then walked over to the right side of the room, providing me with a little more distance from the sinkhole in row three. Yet, even with the shift in where I stood, MAGA found a way to lean his body to see me fully, and for me to see him fully.

Persistent little fucker, I thought.

I started to enter into the forty-five-minute mark of my ninety-minute talk. At this spot, I shared a story about coming out as lesbian and my feelings in my romantic relationship before discovering that I was transgender. When I said the word "lesbian" for the fifteenth time, MAGA nodded to his cohorts, signaling them it was time to leave. The two started standing, but the one on the end remained seated. I knew he wanted to stay. There was something about my story he was connecting with, but due to the prodding from his friends, he joined them. They slowly walked out of the room, making sure that everyone would take in their presence and the leader's hat. When the back door swung closed, the dynamic in the room did a one-eighty. I felt a screen lift from in front of my body. My body became light and my energy started to flow over the space we all shared.

During the evening's question-and-answer segment, I decided to address what had happened. "Some of you in the room may have noticed the young men who left halfway through this talk. A couple of them were softly heckling me as I spoke."

I looked over to the students who had been sitting in front of them. Their heads were doing a slow, but intense, nod in agreement.

"I could have asked them to leave," I said—and then paused—" . . . but I chose not to, because they took the time to come tonight. They sat here in this room with us for forty-five minutes, and I can only hope something I said will have a positive impact on them. We live in a society now where if someone isn't one hundred percent aligned with our views, we write them off. We refuse to listen. We try to find ways to push them out of our spaces. We will not see change if we continue to do this. We'll only see further division."

The audience clapped.

I continually try to challenge myself not to swing to instant judgments about other people based on our differences, especially when it comes to politics. However, encounters like that night's make it hard to stay levelheaded, to be present.

⚠

For the next week, I couldn't shake the image of the leader's face, and the icky feelings that seeped into my skin due to his glares. His eyes were like black holes, trying to suck me into the upside-down world while I dreamed. I do not know what will happen with those three men. I hope that staying firm in my place in front of the room and using my voice in a respectful/nonpolitical tone set an example—not only for them, but also for the others in attendance. I also hope they find what it is they are searching for without harming another human being.

⚠

Two years after my interaction with these young men, national headlines were made when a photo captured a group of young Caucasian teenage boys wearing MAGA hats surrounding an elderly Native American man in Washington, D.C. While there are varying stories regarding what transpired that day, what was consistent for many is that seeing these hats stirred up fear and anger. Since my experience in Texas, I've had other people enter my talks wearing the MAGA hat. The energy in the room becomes stiff as everyone uncomfortably shifts around in their seats.

When this happens, I always work to disarm my anger and fear while I speak. By doing this, I've found that the people who choose to wear the hats are listening. I even made one older man in his red hat smile and laugh. I just keep hoping that we all can continue to listen and that something said will make us less defensive and more willing to reach across the aisle. Our behavior, no matter what side you land on, is becoming so divisive that if we don't change, we'll crumble.

CHAPTER 16

HI, MY NAME IS . . .

Selfie 145 – June 2017

When the calendar flipped to the year 2017, it hit me how that summer would be my twenty-year high-school reunion. It's a cliché, but it's true: As we age, days and years flip by with what feels like a flick of the wrist. With each milestone in life, you begin asking yourself, *How did that happen?!* When I thought about the reunion, it dawned on me, I had now lived the majority of my life outside my hometown and away from the people that created the movielike memories for the first seventeen years of my life. Yes, all those memories wherein I had navigated the world in a female body, known as Kim.

△

Should I put Kim or Ryan . . . or both?

I held the black Sharpie in my hand and looked down at the name tag. I kept staring at the white surface while pondering what my next move should be.

I'll just put Ryan, I thought as I messily scribbled my first name onto the sticky paper.

It felt weird to have to write our names down. The other people I would be coming into contact with weren't strangers; they were people I had spent seventeen years of my life with, from learning how to tie our shoes, to completing complicated math problems. Now, twenty years later, several of us were joining together for our high-school reunion. I stuck the name tag on the left side of my T-shirt, just above my pectoral muscle. I then stood up straight and prepared myself for the unknown of how people would react to my presence.

△

Five months before the event, I had received an invite to join a Facebook group, *Aurora High School Class of '97*. I clicked on the link and read: *What?! It's our 20 Year Class Reunion!!* I went on to read the details and felt grateful to be included in the invite. When my ten-year class reunion had come around, I was two years into my transition. I remember hearing from one of my old classmates that the people in charge were asking how to get ahold of me. At that time, it wasn't completely known that I had transitioned. I didn't receive an invite, and elected not to go, but seeing this invitation was important to me. I saw it as an opportunity to have some closure and healing around how I felt in high school.

The teasing and the comments about my clothes or my physical appearance had been hurtful, but I wanted people to see me now to understand how much internal confusion and struggles I had during that time with all of them. I wanted to show my face and be proud of who I am today, even if it brought about more jokes about me and my identity. I wanted to do it, but I knew I couldn't go alone. Also, I didn't think Lily, who was extremely protective and held no tolerance for offensive comments, would be the right support person to bring to my small town for this gathering.

I didn't have to think long before identifying the perfect sidekick, my friend Sherri. We had first met when she was a new student in my second-grade class in Aurora. The first day that she walked into the room, the teacher instructed her to sit in the desk in front of mine. I spent the rest of the day looking over her shoulder and past her long straw-colored hair. I could sense she was nervous; no one liked being the new kid. The next day, she turned around and looked at me. When my green eyes connected with her brown ones, we formed an instant bond.

Soon photo albums would be filled with pictures of us in a swimming pool or covered in dirt and sweat after a softball game. I couldn't see my life without Sherri in it, but that changed four years later when she shared with me that they were moving away. Her dad, a minister, had been assigned to a new church. My heart wrenched the day I waved good-bye to her and watched her car slowly disappear into the distance.

We were now two hours apart, but the move didn't end our connection. Handwritten letters quickly started to arrive in each of our mailboxes. Instead of closing the letters with a "good-bye," we would both write "let's get together," with hand-drawn music notes next to the scribbled phrase. It was our attempt to replicate the feelings we had about a song performed by Hayley Mills in the movie *The Parent Trap*. We were obsessed with musicals or any movie that had Bette Midler in a leading role.

When I texted her inquiring about her interest in joining me for the high-school reunion, I received an instant response: *Oh my gawd, YES!*

⚠

The day of the reunion, the first stop I made was at her house. Before I could get out of my car, I saw the front door of her house swing open. It felt like we were kids again, waiting with little patience for the other person to arrive. I first saw her husband standing in the entryway, and then Sherri on the stairs of their split-level home. Her eyes were wide open, and the ecstatic energy that I felt from her moved my heart to smile.

Even though it had been twenty-six years since Sherri had lived in Aurora, I knew everyone would recognize her immediately. While she was taller, and her body had shifted from the awkward gangly proportions we all went through with puberty, everything else about her looked exactly the same. She had long medium-blond hair, which framed a face with perfect skin, and a ski-slope nose, thin body, and well-toned muscles. She was basically the type of person that other people hate at a reunion, because even after giving birth to three kids, she looked better now than she had before.

"What do you think of this outfit?" she asked as she ran her hands down either side of her slim torso. I looked at the sheen of her brown spaghetti strap top and sharp lines of her white capris.

"You look great," I said as I started to scan her body. My scan paused when it landed on a pink spot near her right pant pocket. She followed my gaze down to the spot. Her reaction was reactionless.

"Oh! . . . Chapstick . . . in the washing machine, again." She walked over to the kitchen sink and moistened a washcloth to rub on the spot. I still couldn't wrap my head around what life was like being a parent. I felt like we were all too young to have kids, but the reality was most of my classmates would be parents with kids that could be as young as a newborn to age eighteen or a tad older. She tossed the washcloth back onto the kitchen counter and then went around the corner to grab her overnight bag and her own pillow. *Crap, I forgot to bring my own pillow,* I thought. Even though we would be spending the night at my parents' house, it wouldn't be the same place of comfort that I had as a kid.

I let her take the lead out of her entryway and into the warm sun. After hearing both of our seat belts click, I looked over at her. Her eyes were still smiling, and her hands were placed underneath her thighs, with her body leaning forward.

"Are you ready for this?" I asked. It was a question more for myself than for her, the way she was perched on the passenger side made her look like she was just about to take off on a rocket into space rather than a ride two hours west on a flat interstate.

"I'm so excited you asked me. I haven't seen everyone in so long!"

I smiled, still confused by the mixed emotions rumbling around within me. Even though I didn't need driving instructions to Aurora, I placed my phone into a holder, which was clipped into the car's air vent, and pulled up Google Maps. I felt foolish having to pull up navigation in my car in order to find the location of our reunion party. It was being held at the house of one of my classmates—a house I had been to several times during my childhood. Now, though, I had no memories of it or its location. I just knew it sat somewhere on the outskirts of the square-mile grid.

After pulling off the interstate and onto the two-lane highway, I felt my anxiousness begin to stir inside my body. I started to follow the blue line on my GPS, which directed me to turn left onto a county road. Memories I had blocked or that were lost in a fog started to pull up in front of me as we drove past small ranch homes, churches, and ballparks.

The blue line instructed me to take another left. I put my left blinker on and turned onto a gravel road. To the right of us were the county fairgrounds. Old farmhouses were to our left, and open fields, where the occupants of the homes had planted corn or beans, were located behind them. I kept looking past Sherri and out the car window to the fairgrounds. These were grounds we both knew well.

We had run through the old Quonset buildings made out of steel, which were lined up by the entrance. Inside these buildings, our 4-H club participated in singing and dancing competitions. Together, we had sung and danced to many different skits, from the songs "The Candy Man" and "Lollipop" to singing "That's What Friends Are For," in memory of our classmate and fellow 4-H member Megan, who had died in a terrible car accident when we were kids.

These were the same buildings where I gave my first public speech and received the winning award—this was an experience that, to this day, influenced my career as a public speaker. I looked past the steel buildings and saw wood barns and shacks. Under those roofs, I had helped friends show sheep. As we walked the sheep in circles for the judges to look at their build and shape, I would keep thinking, *Watch your feet . . . watch your feet.* Far too many times, my toes, confined within the white tennis shoes we had to wear, would be stomped on by one of the sheep's hooves.

In the middle of the fairgrounds, there were open fields, but one week out of every summer, the field would come alive and be filled with carnival rides and flashing lights. The dollars we had saved from doing household chores would be spent on ride tickets. We would hand those blue tickets to people who had dark tans and deep wrinkles; many had grease or black-ink tattoos scattered across their arms. We would then climb into metal boxes that would spin us around while rotating side to side or up and down. I remembered how sad we were on the day, every year, when we watched the rides being taken down and loaded onto trailers before lining up in a caravan and driving down the highway and onto their next location.

I could feel that sadness again. There were so many moments of joy and feelings of safety that I had had in my small town. Many of these moments and memories had become overshadowed by my feelings of fear, abandonment, and loss of connection. I felt like just seeing the fairgrounds had connected me to something I had lost: the joyful screams as our bodies spun around and around, the eagerness when we waited in line to do it again, the satisfaction in our bellies from the cotton candy that melted in our mouths or stuck to our fingers and lips. I had feared that I would feel foreign to this town, foreign to the land that it was built upon. The farther I drove into this town, the more I knew it would always be my home.

Ahead of us, a red Toyota turned on its right blinker before pulling into a parking lot that was only filled when there were events at the fairgrounds. The fact that there were now several cars there made me feel confident that I could turn off my GPS. We had arrived at the reunion. I turned on my blinker and pulled my Jeep in next to the red car. After shifting into park, I put my hands back at the positions of ten and two on the steering wheel.

I leaned my head forward and looked out over the field of tall grass in front of me. Out of my periphery, to the left, I saw a farmhouse where after softball games I would go for slumber parties. To my left were classmates whom I hadn't seen in twenty years. Some of these classmates had spent our childhood making fun of me, some of them had been close friends, and others were just acquaintances. It can be awkward talking with anyone you haven't seen in a long time; my transition could possibly make it even more awkward. My stomach started to knot up and my breathing quickened in pace.

"Oh, boy," I said.

Sherri reached her left hand out and started to rub my right arm. "It's going to be okay, and if it isn't, we can always leave," she said. "Maybe we should have a code word . . ."

"Guacamole?" I asked, not knowing why out of any code word, that is what came to my mind.

"Guacamole," she said, confirming our safe word and exit plan.

I let out another exhale, looked over to her, and said, "Okay, let's do this."

We both opened our car doors. I swung my feet clad in my favorite pair of cowboy boots onto the ground. When I closed the door, I felt a breeze blowing in from the south. The chill made me happy with my decision to wear blue jeans instead of shorts. Usually, by the middle of June, it was humid and sticky, especially next to fields, but this year had been unusually cold. Along with jeans, I wore my favorite blue T-shirt. It fit me like a second skin in my shoulders, bicep, and chest, but hung loose around my torso. While my body had changed, my clothing choices had remained the same, jeans and a T-shirt. The only thing different is that these clothes were worn to show my body, instead of the jeans and T-shirts I wore in high school that were purposefully too big in order to hide the body underneath.

Sherri came around the back side of the car and we both started walking, side by side. I loved the feel of gravel and the sound it made under my boots. It brought me a sense of comfort, a sense of belonging, and returning to a place I had come from but lost.

We stopped and looked both ways before crossing the road and walking up to the house. When we started up the driveway, I caught brief glimpses at the small number of faces that had also arrived on time. *What if I don't recognize anyone? What if I've forgotten someone's name?* Getting closer, I saw the blank name tags scattered out on a table. I felt relieved, but also sad. The majority of us had spent eighteen years together, from preschool and kindergarten to the day we moved our tassels from one side of the square hat on our head to the other. Now we were writing our names down and gathering like strangers at a conference.

After writing *Ryan* on my name tag, I straightened my back and turned around. I instantly made eye contact with a face I knew. *Brad. His name is Brad,* I thought.

"Hey, Ryan!" he said in a welcoming and friendly voice. To have the first classmate I came into contact with use my name without any sign of hesitation or awkwardness helped ease my nerves.

"Hey, Brad!" I said while extending my right hand for a firm handshake. When we were kids, he would have been considered one of the "cool kids" in our class. While I was in all of the activities with the "cool kids," I wasn't part of the club. Standing there, talking with him like I would any adult, I realized that, along with my nervousness around my transition, I had to let go of my teenage brain's perception of people and the hierarchies we had formed. We were all nearing our forties, but my brain wanted to put us back to our late teens and our naivety.

Knowing that my brain was having trouble catching up to how all of us have changed, I began to wonder how people's brains were working when looking at me. No longer did I have shoulder-length, curly hair. No longer did I have a female shape. No longer did I have the name Kim.

More classmates started walking up the driveway as the sun was slowly starting its descent for the evening. I turned with Brad to acknowledge the new arrivals.

"Hey, John!" Brad said to a former classmate who looked almost exactly the same as he had when we were kids. His blond hair was still cut short, but now receding, and his body's build was still small and slim. His blue eyes were still just as kind and gentle. He walked up and shook Brad's hand and then looked at me. I shook his hand, watching his eyes glance down to my name tag.

"Hey, I am Ryan," I said to him.

"Oh, okay," he said in his gentle voice. I could see the confusion on his face. He had no clue who I was. The news about my transition apparently hadn't made it to his farm in a town outside of Aurora. We continued to shake hands, and I knew the next question he was going to ask would be "Are you married to someone here?"

Instead of waiting for him to ask, I leaned down to him. He was one of the shorter guys in our class, and I said, "I used to be Kim . . . I know it's a little awkward." Then I let out one of my classic nervous giggles.

His eyes locked on mine and I could tell he was starting to put the pieces together. "Oh! No one had told me . . . I didn't know," he said. We released the handshake, and we both laughed. He took another second to look at me, and I knew his brain was still processing everything. I wondered how many other folks hadn't heard, and if they hadn't, I could only hope they would be as kind and gentle as John.

"We should have some beer," I said to break any chance for more awkwardness. Behind us, to my chagrin, there was a keg filled with Bud Light. At that point, I could have used a higher alcohol-content beer with some flavor, but I knew I should just be grateful to have something cold and wet. I grabbed a red plastic cup and then realized I had never drunk a beer in a big party setting with my classmates.

Of course, one person I had drunk a beer with was Sherri. One night during a sleepover, I snuck two cans of Coors Light out of my parents' basement refrigerator. Sherri and I chugged them as fast as we could. We had heard if you chug them, you get drunk faster. A few wine coolers had also entered my bedroom, but otherwise I avoided drinking and any scene where it would be involved. Looking down at the keg in front of me, I also realized this would only be the third time in life I've primed a keg's pump. I reached down and placed my hand on the black knob. My arm moved up and down as I watched the pale liquid fill the cup. With beer in hand, I knew my social anxiety would slowly fade away as the night moved forward.

More of my female classmates started to arrive. I realized I had first started talking with the men in my class, which was interesting, since they weren't the ones I had hung out with in my childhood and teenage years. Each time I saw the face of one of the girls, now women, that I had grown up with, I would be greeted with a warm "Hey, Ryan" and an authentic hug. When one of the moms that had been my softball coach came out and hugged me, I felt hope.

It was another moment in my life where I had to check my own assumptions. It was a moment that reminded me of the goodness in people, regardless of what size town they lived in or their political affiliation. It gave me hope that the more people have relationships with folks who have different lives and identities from their own, the more we can appreciate and respect our uniqueness and our differences. In our attempt to bring more equality to our country, we've become so divisive toward anything or anyone that is different from our exact views, we are counterproductively creating more separation.

A tall and slightly heavier man walked up with his wife. I knew right away he was my best friend, Matt, from when we were little kids. We had lived close to each other in the country and had bonded over Superman. I was always jealous over his Superman shirt, which had Velcro for the cape to attach to. I had always just tied a red handkerchief or dishcloth around my neck for my cape. I'll never forget the day my mom made me a Superman shirt with the cape sewn into it. When I got to wear this homemade outfit, my imagination believed that my flying was better and faster than Matt's, since I never lost my cape from being snagged on a corner and getting ripped away from the Velcro.

"Hey, Ryan," he said. We shook hands. I could tell it was a little hard for him to see me. "You know, my mom still has in her house a framed picture of us in our Superman shirts."

"That's great. I thought about wearing a Superman shirt tonight . . . but . . ." I trailed off. I had no clue where I was going with sharing my outfit contemplation. While we had been close as little kids, we slipped apart with each year that had passed. We did date each other in middle school. By "dating," I mean on Valentine's Day I gave him a bundle of eight

Tootsie Pops as a gift. He had picked me up a box of fancy chocolates from a trip with his parents, but ended up eating them on the way home.

During our junior year of high school, we also went to prom together. I had always had a crush on him, so to go with him to prom was surreal. Now we stood next to each other and I could only wonder what feelings he had from seeing his junior-prom date as a man with a beard.

As we started to walk into the house to fill our plates with pork chops, mashed potatoes, and fruit salad (a classic small-town meal), he said, "I got to admit, this is kind of weird."

I just shook my head. "Life has been a wild ride, Matt."

After dinner, a photographer from the town's newspaper came to snap a class photo. Out of the eighty-six people who were part of the Class of '97, only twenty-four of us came to the twenty-year class reunion. We lined up in three small rows on top a metal picnic table and bench to pose. Wives and husbands stood behind the photographer and also snapped pictures of us, which were then quickly texted to other people.

When the photographer dropped the camera from his face, he said, "Don't move yet. I need to get all of your names to go in the order that you are sitting." He slowly made his way down the rows and lines. When he got to me, I said, "My name is Ryan Sallans."

I smiled, thinking about my picture being in the paper with my name. As a teenager, my face was a frequent image in the paper because of all the different activities that I had participated in. I wondered what the townspeople would say when they looked at our black-and-white photo and saw me there. It made me sad to think that many people may not know who any of us were. Another cruel thing about time, our names and faces fade away and new ones take their places.

The sun had completely tucked away for the night, and the moon took over dimly lighting the ground and people's faces. We all stood around the aboveground swimming pool flanked by tiny strings of lights. Bats began to visit us. As they swooped over our heads, we watched them dip into the pool for a tiny drink. Everyone continued to stand around one another, sharing stories about their careers, kids, and different life adventures. I didn't have to use the code word "guacamole," but I wanted to begin saying good-byes and head to my parents' house before they went to bed. John walked up to me before I could to him. He was closer to his rounds of good-byes than I was.

166

"Thank you for coming tonight," he said before giving me a hug. He was the first and only guy I had hugged at the reunion. His gesture was one of the highlights of the night.

⚠

Time moves in a way where our brain and memories keep seeing us at one point, but our bodies are moving at a different pace, on a different plane. Driving Sherri back home the next day, I felt a form of peacefulness and clarity wash over me as my Jeep went down the highway lined on either side by cornfields with stalks coming up to hip height. I thought back to when I was a kid out in those cornfields, pulling tassels off the female corn to prevent cross-pollination. Looking down at the road we were driving on, I thought back to the six summers I spent between college semesters working on the State Road Department crew, where I helped lay down the asphalt, install the road signs, and mow the ditches. The memories washed over me, reconnecting my old self with my new self.

Driving down the interstate, we passed the city of Lincoln, the city where I first lay on the ground dying from anorexia nervosa, only to get back up and begin to face what scared me the most. Memories of each step I took in my recovery, and watching my body change from being emaciated to full, from Kim to then Ryan, flashed through my mind like a slide show set to change images every two seconds. An hour later, we were back in Omaha. I dropped Sherri off at her home and then headed to the place I've planted my roots. I started to sort out all the different memories and emotions washing over me.

Going to the reunion set my life into the next plane of motion. I knew then that as I moved into my forties, it wouldn't be about separating out each part of who I had been. Rather, I should join them together and allow myself to feel the emotions from every trail I've walked. Doing this would allow me to start my new journey in life, learning how to care for my body and my health, while healing past traumas and confronting the new challenges that lay ahead.

I am no longer categorizing myself as Dr. Sallans's daughter, the patient with an eating disorder, or trans man Ryan. My professional life as a transgender speaker has kept me deeply entrenched within my trans identity, but in my personal life I am undergoing a new transition. This one goes beyond surgery, hormones, or moments that I've had to come out. This new transition swipes away my identities and dives into my mortality, as well as my relationship with everything that surrounds me. I am searching the undefined.

EPILOGUE

TRANSEXUAL MENACE

Selfie 150 – November 2017

Hey you, how do you feel about writing the quote for the Transgender Day of Remembrance Memorial Cenotaph Statue we are dedicating in November? I had to re-read the request and check who the sender was. It came from a transgender woman who was the director of the Transgender Community Coalition of Palm Springs, California. I was hesitant to reply, since I still had PTSD over the online attack I had received for speaking on the same day as TDOR in Missouri the year before. The past year, however, had taught me that when we let bullies and assumptions intimidate us, it prevents us, and those around us, from moving forward.

The past year, I had seen a rebirth of my relationship with my parents and classmates. It was now time to have a rebirth within the transgender community and overcome the belief that I had nothing to contribute to a day like TDOR. I needed to recognize that people valued my work, my voice, and my approach to advocating for the transgender community, so I pushed past the fear of being attacked and accepted the request.

In order to provide a quote for the cenotaph, I first had to look up what that word even meant. I learned that a cenotaph is a monument for a person buried elsewhere. Next I read the story about the young transgender woman that the statue was memorializing. On a Thursday morning in 2014 in Fort Myers, Florida, police officers found the body of Yaz'min Sanchez, a transgender woman, who was murdered by first being shot and then set on fire behind a garbage bin in an alley. The cenotaph to memorialize her was a sculpture of a body lying on its side on the ground, covered by butterflies getting ready to take flight. Reading about Yaz'min and then seeing the picture of the statue made me stumble back and pause. The way the light shimmered off the metal wings made everything around the statue feel alive.

I realized that being asked to provide a quote for the plaque was a huge honor, and something I needed to make sure spoke to honoring Yaz'min and the thousands of others we lose in the transgender community due to hate, violence, and power. I also thought about the importance of TDOR not only being an event to remember those we have lost, but it should be an event to pull us together so we can recognize the value and beauty in how our differences make us a vibrant community. When we hear each other's stories, we need to go past the surface and dive into the soul.

For Yaz'min, for other victims, and for survivors, I decided to write:

Hate and violence will not erase the beauty of our individuality. Even with death, our love will carry us through the winds and into beating hearts, where we'll be held and passed to future generations.

After finishing the quote, I offered to come and speak at the event without a speaker's fee. I felt it was important for me to speak, to hold a candle for all the people we have lost, and to continue memorializing Brandon Teena through sharing stories of his life and death.

△

On November 20, 2017, I stepped up to the podium and looked out at the crowd gathered on the steps of the City Hall in Palm Springs. The sun had set, but I could see everyone's faces through the shimmer of the candles they held in their hands. These were all faces that were solemnly hopeful. I was the last speaker for the evening.

Behind me stood Gwendolyn Ann Smith, the founder of the "Remember Our Dead" project, which is now TDOR. I wondered how she felt standing there and not only seeing the large number of attendees for the Palm Springs' event, but to scroll through all the events that now take place around the world for TDOR. Standing next to Gwendolyn was Ian Harvie. I hadn't seen him since we had both appeared on the Trisha

Goddard show. It felt good to see him again, and to be standing alongside him. It is amazing how you can find comfort without even speaking words with a person who has walked different but also similar paths.

I looked back out to the crowd and spoke to the importance of us working together to end violence, by first working to build bridges in the community instead of marginalizing one another. How do we expect to see change and end the fighting, when we can't even get along with one another? I then pulled out my candle and set it on top of the podium.

"Tonight, with this candle, I want to also remember Brandon Teena, who lost his life due to ignorance and violence in Nebraska on December 31, 1993. I honor him because he was a fellow Nebraskan that was a victim not only to violence, but to the ignorance of a medical community that didn't have the knowledge or resources equipped to help him honor his identity. Transgender Day of Remembrance is an important day to raise awareness of these injustices and to work to try and improve safety for our transgender sisters and brothers, but it is also a time for us to recognize the beautiful lives that continue to thrive in society and culture. It is hopefully a way that we can encourage more days to be created that will honor the beauty and not just the pain—the pride, and not just the injustice. It is time that we do what we can to start painting new pictures and narratives for everyone in our community.

"Every day there is something amazing happening in the life of someone that identifies as transgender, whether it is: announcing their love for someone else, starting on hormones to start seeing their gender transform for others to see, receiving the court order from a judge that allows them to change their legal name, or changing their IDs to match their identity. Everything that happens to affirm a person's life and identity has come from people speaking out, seeking acceptance, and working toward policy change.

"Through having events that allow for education, celebration, and bridging of communities, we create something stronger and more supportive for all of us who have been victims of harassment and discrimination. By remembering those before us, we'll also never forget where we have come from, and what we need to do, to strive for a more accepting tomorrow."

As I finished my speech, the audience clapped—a sign that something I had said resonated. I grabbed my candle and stepped back in line with the other speakers. I let out a big breath, speaking at these events is nerve-wracking. Gwendolyn leaned over to me and whispered, "I have a story I want to share with you after this is over."

I nodded back at her, hoping I didn't say something at TDOR that was inaccurate.

Lights started to flash as one of the organizers placed her hand on the blanket that covered the cenotaph. Slowly she pulled the large blue quilt off the butterflies' wings, revealing the statue to the audience for the first time. People started to slowly walk up and place their candles around Yaz'min's statue before turning their heads down, closing their eyes, and saying a few words. After people were able to spend time with the statue, honoring Yaz'min's life, speakers and attendees then gathered around the cenotaph to pose for pictures. When the crowd started to thin, Gwendolyn walked up to me.

"So, in your speech, you mentioned Brandon Teena. I wanted to share with you that it was partly because of Brandon that TDOR is what it is today," she said with an encouraging smile.

"Really?" I asked, slightly in shock.

"Yes, in 1998 the documentary about Brandon was showing at a theater in the Castro in San Francisco. A bunch of us that went decided to write the names of transgender people who had been murdered on posters and hold them up outside the theater before the film started. So, in a way, Brandon's story inspired how we do TDOR today."

I got tears in my eyes when I heard Gwendolyn share that story. My heart started to feel different strings attaching my spirit with others around the nation and the world in ways I didn't think was possible. Her story also reinforced the importance of remembering people, for even in their passing, they are still an influence. I wiped the tears from my eyes and saw another trans woman walking up to me. She was wearing a black button-up jacket, her long blond hair covered the back.

"I want to show you something," she said, then turned around and pulled her hair to the side. On the back, in capital white and red letters, her jacket said, TRANSEXUAL MENACE. More tears came to my eyes.

I had never seen one of the jackets in person. However, I had seen pictures of people from around the nation wearing those jackets and T-shirts, with the alternative spelling, while standing on the steps of the Richardson County Courthouse in Falls City, Nebraska. They had assembled to protest the crimes of the two men who were on trial for the rape and murder of Brandon.

In the '90s, the jackets and T-shirts were a way for folks who "you wouldn't know are transgender" to be visible and to point out how ridiculous it was to be scared of us. Noticing the need to end the stigma around being transsexual, chapters began to pop up around the United States. On each jacket, beneath TRANSEXUAL MENACE, the city where the chapter was founded was embroidered.

"Oh, wow," I said as I touched the jacket. Her jacket had *Suffolk L.I.* (for Long Island) embroidered underneath. "Would it be okay if I tried it on?"

"Of course!" she said before starting to pull on the sleeves.

I smiled as I slipped the jacket over my arms. It felt amazing to be wearing a part of history, but it also made me feel a little unsettled. I imagined how scary it would have been to wear the TRANSEXUAL MENACE T-shirts and jackets out in public—especially during a time where being transgender was still widely ignored and dismissed. During that era, there weren't *any* protections at all, making the risks for mistreatment, discrimination, and violence even higher.

Recognizing what past generations have gone through to get us where we are today is one of the reasons why I do not see myself as a trailblazer for issues that impact someone who is transgender. I see myself more as a trail maintainer. The paths have already been created, I just make sure they aren't forgotten and that they retain integrity. There may be a few offshoots on these trails that I've routed along the way, but I don't need credit or an award. Those accolades would just stay with me; I'd rather just keep seeing people able to live their lives and be treated with respect along the way.

Wearing the jacket and being appreciative of what people who are transgender have gone through before me, I felt another bridge being built within me. It joined me to the bigger picture of trans rights, activism, and advocacy. I can only hope that through my stories I can create more bridges linking the younger generations with those that fought to get us where we are today. I can only hope that I can help us move away from focusing on everything wrong about a person's appearance or the language they use, to asking: What is it that connects us? What is it that we can learn from one another?

For me as an individual, as I move through my forties, I plan to assemble all of my pieces and recognize that I am more than a man. I am a human being. Like anyone else, I am trying to find my footing and how I can help in this challenging world. I know that I will keep stumbling, I will not be perfect, and that I cannot be everything for everyone. None of us can. What we can do, though, is thank a person for showing up, and then give them a hug.

ABOUT THE AUTHOR

Ryan K. Sallans is a Nebraska native who resides in Omaha. He graduated Sigma Tau Delta from the University of Nebraska-Lincoln with a Bachelor of Arts in anthropology and English, Master of Arts in English, and Master of Arts in educational psychology.

Sallans is the author of *Second Son: Transitioning Toward My Destiny, Love and Life*. He has written essays and forewords for the books *The Gender Quest Workbook, Manning Up: Transsexual Men on Finding Brotherhood, Family & Themselves*, and *My Body, My Words*.

He has published the books *What's Normal Anyway? A comic about being trans male* and *OUTsider: Crossing Borders. Breaking Rules. Gaining Pride.*

Along with writing, Sallans travels the nation as a professional speaker where he provides keynotes, presentations and training to corporations, health care institutions, federal agencies, nonprofit organizations, and colleges and universities. You can learn more about him and his work by visiting his website: RyanSallans.com, or by following him on social media underneath the handle: Ryan Sallans.

Photo by Melanie Rose Smith

Also by Ryan K. Sallans:

Second Son: Transitioning Toward My Destiny, Love and Life

Other Scout Publishing Titles:

OUTsider: Crossing Borders. Breaking Rules. Gaining Pride.
by Ruth Marimo

What's Normal Anyway? A comic about being trans male
by Morgan Boecher

scoutpublishingllc.com

ACKNOWLEDGMENTS

As a writer who works in the realm of nonfiction, I give readers a very deep and intimate look into not just my life, but those that are also close to me. It is sometimes tricky because I am sharing my own perception and memories of events and how that has impacted or influenced my next actions. I am very grateful to everyone in this book, even those that have not been kind to me. After all, being challenged is something that helps all of us with growth.

I recognize that for people written about in this book, you are going along with me on this ride and being written about from my perspective. I know that if you were to write the same story, it would look different due to your own memories and experiences. I can only hope my storytelling can provide space for healing and expansion for all of us and for readers.

I want to thank my best friend and wife, Lily, for making me a better human and for standing by my side as my biggest supporter. I wouldn't be here without you. As Alexi Murdoch says in his song "Orange Sky": "In your love, my salvation lies."

I also want to thank my family. I learn something new about myself and about you with each year that passes.

My books and my story could never be what they have become without the knowledge, guidance, insight, and creativity of my designer and art director, Erika Block, and my editor, Stephanie Finnegan. I would be absolutely lost without the both of you.

Being someone that loves looking at pictures—I have a lot of photo albums—I want to thank the photographers that have helped shape this book and also my life: Aidan Faiella with Faiella Studios, Fred Schneider, and Melanie Rose Smith. I also want to thank Hunter Lea, the photos you took at Lily's and my wedding are absolutely stunning.

TRANSFORMING MANHOOD

Thank you to Jason Robert Ballard with *FTM Magazine* for starting the "What Trans Looks Like" campaign, and for the T-shirts with that slogan. I am wearing one of these shirts in the photo on the front cover, you can grab your own at: whattranslookslike.com.

Thank you to everyone who has read chapters, reviewed copies, and provided me with your insight: Loren Kleinman, Diane Anderson-Minshall, Florence Rosiello-Chevalier, Jesi DeWitt, Julie Dierberger, Anneliese Singh, Diane Ehrensaft and Robin Zagurski.

Thank you to everyone who has hosted me as a speaker at your events. You have shaped a large part of my life, and a larger understanding of humanity.

Lastly, thank you to my readers. You have gone on this journey with me, and I greatly appreciate your support, while also hoping you understand more about yourself through my stories.